PLAIN
TALK
ON
Hebrews

D0168531

BOOKS BY DR. GUTZKE . . .

PLAIN TALK ON

Hebrews

MANFORD GEORGE GUTZKE
PH.D.

Lamplighter Books Grand Rapids, Michigan
Zondervan Publishing House

PLAIN TALK ON HEBREWS

© 1976 by The Zondervan Corporation

Grand Rapids, Michigan

Lamplighter Books are published by Zondervan Publishing House, 1415 Lake Drive, S.E., Grand Rapids, Michigan 49506

ISBN 0-310-25541-4

Library of Congress Cataloging in Publication Data

Gutzke, Manford George.
  Plain talk on Hebrews.

  1. Bible.   N. T. Hebrews—Commentaries.   I. Title.
BS2775.3.G87   227'.87'07   75-21129

Printed in the United States of America

    84   85   86   87   88 — 10   9

CONTENTS

196⊕3

INTRODUCTION

Do you realize God reveals more through Jesus Christ than had been revealed in the Scriptures of the Old Testament?

> God, who at sundry times and in divers manners spake in time past unto the fathers by the prophets, hath in these last days spoken unto us by his Son (Heb. 1:1-2).

These are the first words in the Epistle to the Hebrews, a manuscript written by a minister of Christ to believers who had accepted Him, and this brings to mind the question as to why anyone would write to people who already believe? Shall we find here some argument of proof that they were right in believing? What shall we look for? Let us look first at the title itself: We call it The Epistle to the Hebrews and we could ask ourselves who these Hebrews were. They are never referred to in the epistle itself and there is no point at which there is a definition given or information as to who these people were who were called The Hebrews.

Is there a chance such people are among us today? We have in mind that Abraham was the first Hebrew, and the followers of Abraham, especially the members of his family, would naturally be called Hebrews. In this book the use of the term is obscure, but we know that it was written to people who were believers, people who were instructed in the Old Testament Scriptures and based their thinking on them. Inasmuch as that was the case, they knew the law of Moses; they knew what God required of man. They had accepted the call of God as being real and had committed themselves to obeying the call, the law of God and the commandments of God.

This epistle was the Word of God to these believers who knew the law, who knew what God requires of man. It was written because apparently there was danger a believer might stop at this point and not mature in his faith. This is a dangerous position, one that denies a Christian what God has intended for him.

Suppose a person decided to have a garden. First, he would get a plot of ground; then he would plant seeds in it. There are people who do not do any more than that, and of course the result of such a procedure is failure. People will often start to do something, and will then be tempted to think they have done it. No, there is a bit of distance between deciding to have a garden, and getting the land and seed and actually *having* the garden. The seed must be planted and then cultivated.

Believers may receive Christ Jesus as Savior and yet need to realize that He is Lord. They may not be so ready to follow Him as Lord. Another way in which this truth I am speaking of can be illustrated is like this: The wedding of two young people could be wonderful, but if they stopped there it would not be satisfactory. The wedding itself may be a grand occasion, but what does it mean? The wedding is the beginning of married life, and far more goes on than just what happened at the wedding. So it is with believers in Christ. They may have lived through a period of time in which they have thought about the Lord and wondered about Him. Finally they have agreed to accept the Lord's proposal, and now they belong to Him (as the girl when she puts on the engagement ring). By accepting Christ these believers indicate they now belong to the Lord, and they intend to live with Him. But if they never do any more they will miss everything. They are like a person who becomes engaged but never marries. Before long such a girl would be unhappy, and everyone would say she was in an unsatisfactory situation.

Now with believers this is also true. To have in our hearts and minds the conviction that Christ Jesus is the Savior, and to know that God would work to save, to ask him to do so and then not follow through would be damaging to our spiritual experience. To receive Christ as Lord means that I would need more understanding of the Scriptures. This is implied in the first verse of the Epistle to the Hebrews. "God, who at sundry times and in divers manners spake in time past unto the fathers by the prophets, hath in these last days spoken unto us by his Son." In the following context we are told how the Son of God was more important than those who had gone before. The Epistle to the Hebrews was written to teach the deeper meanings of the gospel that go beyond the matter of accepting the Lord. When we say, "God has spoken," we must have in mind this is a revelation from God; He does have a message for us. "Unto the fathers" brings to mind the blessings we receive from believers of times past. Ours is a wonderful heritage from believers of former times, and the reason we are as blessed as we are now at this stage in the Christian church and as Christian people is because of those who have lived before and left us the benefits of their experience. "God has spoken unto the fathers" (the people who have gone before) "by the prophets" (men like Moses and others who interpreted the Word and the will of God).

It was these prophets primarily who gave us the Old Testament, which was true and eternal. But there was more to come, as we read in verse 2: "Hath in these last days spoken unto us by his Son." "These last days" means this generation, at this time. I am not sure the word "last" refers to the end of the world. It does not mean last in the sense of all time, but last in the sense of all the time until now. This is the last phase — contemporary and now. "Hath in these last days spoken to us" reminds us that God communicates His will apart from the natural processes.

Through nature we can sense the existence of God, but we can't learn about the gospel because it is not to be found in nature which we can see. When we say that God has spoken to us through His Son we do not mean He has spoken to us through the stars or the plants or the animals, the storms at sea or the events of history. We mean He has spoken to us by the incarnation of Jesus Christ, by Jesus of Nazareth, His Son, and this is the supreme revelation. God has communicated His will by the prophets — those who were sent with a message — but in these last days He has communicated His will to us by sending His Son. He will tell us who this Son is and how important it is for us to believe how significant He was. The great truth we should note here is that beyond what is revealed in the Old Testament, there is more in the New Testament; beyond what we have in the law, there is more in grace; and beyond what we have by the messengers of the Word of God in the Old Testament, we have the Son of God in the New Testament. That is what we shall be learning about in this epistle. Just now the writer is interested in impressing upon his readers that they should give special heed to what the Son has said, because He is more important than those who have gone before Him.

PLAIN
TALK
ON
Hebrews

Chapter 1

THE SON IS GREATER THAN ANGELS

Do you think angels are real beings?

Being made so much better than the angels, as he hath by inheritance obtained a more excellent name than they (Heb. 1:4).

In verses 4-14 we learn that Christ, the Son of God, is better than the angels who are the servants of God. The Old Testament reveals truth about angels. It is amazing in reading the Bible to note how little personal description there is about these beings. Angels are mentioned from time to time in different Scriptures, and they were always messengers. There is no description of their appearance. This makes one think the term "angels" is more functional than it is descriptive; it has more reference to what they did than what they looked like. We are to understand these angels brought the message of God, and they continue to do so. Some people may wonder whether anyone who is a messenger is an angel. That may be all this word means, but that view is not quite adequate for indicating the meaning of the Bible usage. In the Scriptures some of these beings came in the form of men to bring messages, and would then be taken away or would act in some way that would be quite different from the behavior of an ordinary human being.

The Hebrews believed in angels and recognized that these angels were persons who brought the Word of God to them, because no human being ever in himself came to the conclusion by reflection that the law of God was true or that it meant this and that. No, such insight was revealed from heaven. God revealed His message to man. There is something about the grace of God that no human being can ever imagine; God has to show it to him.

The message of God as seen in the Bible is set forth in two sections — the Old and the New Testaments. Generally speaking, we say the Old Testament presents the Law, the Ten Commandments, the judgments, and so on. It largely sets forth what God requires of man in order to have God's blessing. In the New Testament we think of grace as over against the law in the Old Testament. This grace is the function of the Lord Jesus Christ. And so, while we have in the Bible both the Old and the New Testaments — one is preparatory and the other manifestation — the difference between the two is that the manifestation is more important than the preparation.

This truth can be illustrated in this way: If you think of the Old Testament as a map to direct you in your travels, the New Testament is like a guide who will lead you along the way. One can think of the Old Testament as being a prescription that would tell you when and how to take the medicine, but the New Testament presents the doctor, and the doctor is better than the prescription. He may write the prescription but he is better. Or we could think of a person having repair work done. In the Old Testament he would be given a box of tools and perhaps even a book of instructions, but in the New Testament the mechanic is presented to you. The mechanic may use the Old Testament tools and book of instructions, but he knows what needs to be done, and can build what is in his mind apart from those tools. What we have in the Old Testament is true and good, but what we have in the New Testament is also true and better — like a guide is better than a map, like a doctor is better than a prescription, and like a mechanic is better than tools and instructions.

The Scripture urges us to remember that the Son is better than the messengers, the angels who helped make God's law known to man. His Word that He speaks to us in grace should actually be given preferential hearing because of who He is.

> For unto which of the angels said he at any time, Thou art my Son, this day have I begotten thee? And again, I will be to him a Father, and he shall be to me a Son? (Heb. 1:5).

Jesus Christ was actually the Son of God, and angels were told to worship Him. "And let all the angels of God worship him" (Heb. 1:6). The Son of God is also declared to be the King:

> But unto the Son he saith, Thy throne, O God, is for ever and ever (Heb. 1:8).

He actually is to be King and the angels are to be His servants . . . "Who maketh his angels spirits, and his ministers a flame of fire" (Heb. 1:7). (The word "ministers" means servants).

And, Thou, Lord, in the beginning hast laid the foundation of the earth; and the heavens are the works of thine hands (Heb. 1:10).

This indicates that the Lord Jesus Christ as the Son of God is the Creator, and it is He who made earth and Heaven. He made all things. The writer goes on to point out that He is eternal:

They shall perish; but thou remainest; and they all shall wax old as doth a garment; and as a vesture shalt thou fold them up, and they shall be changed: but thou art the same, and thy years shall not fail (Heb. 1:11-12).

The Son of God is shown to be at the right hand of God, waiting until His enemies are subdued, while causing the angels to function to serve the heirs of salvation:

But to which of the angels said he at any time, Sit on my right hand, until I make thine enemies thy footstool? (Heb. 1:13).

These were God's words to His Son whose purpose was far greater than that of the angels because He had come to fulfill the law and to provide a means for keeping that law. The law of God, which is elementary in all religious truth, and original because it comes from God Himself, and fundamental to all spiritual truth, would never be changed because it is grounded in the very nature of God. Our Lord Jesus Christ said in Matthew 5:17-20 that not one jot or tittle would pass from the law until all was fulfilled. He honored and respected the law but He was able to remove it as an obstacle between believers and God by fulfilling it, and He provided for believers a way to come to God.

The Old Testament admonishes a person to do right, but the New Testament will call the believer to come to God and He will help him to do right. The law was good even though men could never keep it, but Christ Jesus is better because He is able to bring believers past the law of God.

Chapter 2

THE REVELATION BY THE SON IS MORE IMPORTANT THAN THE LAW

Do you realize there is more to being right with God than acknowledging what is right and doing it?

> Therefore we ought to give the more earnest heed to the things which we have heard, lest at any time we should let them slip (Heb. 2:1).

Here the writer of Hebrews is emphasizing that God, who spoke in times past to the fathers through the prophets has in these last days spoken to us through His Son. Since the Lord Jesus Christ is much better than any of the messengers who had come before, believers should give His words special heed. It is common understanding that if a man does right, God will bless him. Almost everyone realizes that no one can really do all that is right and good, and this often frustrates many people so that they give up at the very beginning. But that is not necessary. The gospel of Jesus Christ tells the sinner, the person who is not doing what is right, how he can come to God.

What it means to do right in the sight of God is set forth in the Old Testament by the prophets, by the Ten Commandments, and by all the interpretations given by various messengers who were called angels. For many this is the content of the gospel, and there is much real truth here. But there is more to be done than just what the law requires. In the Old Testament there is a clear presentation of the reality of God, of the eternal nature of His law, and of our responsibility to obey Him, and this never varies. This whole truth simply emphasizes that whatsoever a man soweth, that shall he also reap. In Christ Jesus we have learned how a believer can sow and be blessed, yet his responsibility is still to obey God. The believer is not only able to obey Him by doing what God wants him to do, but also he can obey by receiving what God wants to give him. This is presented in the gospel.

In the Old Testament is revealed the truth of the reality of heaven. The reality of the spiritual world and the reality of man's soul are very important. These truths are basic and they are needed to enable anyone to understand the life in Christ Jesus. In the Old Testament the soul is brought face to face with the reality of angels — actual created beings who live in another world and who do the will of God. The very fact that there were angels, as messengers of God, implies that God had a will that was to be revealed. The Old Testament indicates this. God is the Creator of the heavens and earth, a living, active God, almighty and powerful. He has His eye upon men for good, and He has a will for men to follow that will lead them into blessing. The believer will heed that will.

As we read and meditate upon the Old Testament we see the reality of the will of God. He is not a star that we should look at; He is not a picture we could hang upon the wall. God is a living being — the Creator and Keeper of the whole world. This God has a plan for man, an actual, real plan, that He intends to carry out. Believers should be ready to do His will. All of this is found in the Old Testament, where we can see the reality of our responsibility to do His will. There is severe judgment upon our actions should we fail to respond to Him. It is written into the very nature of things that man is responsible for his conduct. All our government constitutions bear this idea in mind. Man can understand the law and he is responsible if he breaks it.

All of this is Old Testament revelation, yet all of it is also found in the gospel. This is what was preached by John the Baptist. This is what was meant by "God spake in time past unto the fathers by the prophets." He did not tell them a half-truth; what He told them was true. Believers who live on this side of Calvary are now challenged to realize that God said more by His Son than He said in the Old Testament days through the messengers.

What else can we learn through the Son of God? We can discover something about our guilt and about our doom. We are now under condemnation because we have committed sin, but our guilt can be removed by His grace in Christ Jesus who died for us as the perfect, eternal sacrifice on our behalf. This language may be difficult to understand, I know, but it *can* be understood, and it is meaningful. The guilt of the sinner can be taken away through the Lord Jesus Christ. The New Testament reveals the truth that we can be born again by His Word and by His power when we repudiate the flesh with all of its proclivity to sin. We can be set free from the flesh, because we can be raised again in the Spirit. The Spirit accepts and receives the things that pertain to God and is sensitive to Him. We can open our hearts to receive the Holy Spirit and His power through the grace of God.

We find this in the New Testament through the Son of God, the Lord

Jesus Christ. It does not change what we have already learned: The law is still the law; heaven is still real; God is still real and the angels are still real. Our responsibility to do the will of God still holds true, but now we find that Christ Jesus has made it possible for us to be reconciled to God in spite of our sin, and to be born again as new creatures who have the grace of God operative in them. We are still called upon to obey His will but now we have His Spirit within us, moving us into willing obedience. The Christian person has the very happy experience of actually being carried along in the will of God to want to do His will. It is a joy to the believer to do what God wants to have done.

This grace of God needs to be received by us as we listen and give earnest heed to the things that were spoken of by the Lord Jesus Christ. We believe in Him and as a result He works in us. This is a great truth. It is true, as the Old Testament states, that the law of God is everlasting, and man will come before God to be judged for deeds done in the body. Heaven is real. God exercises a judgmental attitude and observation in overseeing all His creatures on the face of the earth. But in the new covenant, God in grace and mercy and love has provided through Christ Jesus the ability to move toward certain goals. It is essential to our spiritual experience that we respond to the grace of God by believing in Jesus Christ and in what He says. This is why we go into all the world to teach that stealing is wrong and killing is wrong. But we also need to go and tell them that God will forgive them in Christ Jesus — that a change will take place, and the grace of God will work in their hearts. That is the truth revealed in Christ Jesus.

Chapter 3

THE PERIL OF NEGLECT

How shall we escape, if we neglect so great salvation? (Heb. 2:3).

Do you realize that I can neglect only what I already own?

For years I thought this question was a warning to unbelievers, indicating that any person who had not accepted Christ should face the fact that he would not escape if he neglected this great salvation. All of that is true, but close attention to the context and careful reflection upon the meaning of the words leads me to say this is a message to believers.

I had a garden in the days during the war when we called them "victory gardens." During the hot days of summer there were times I did not want to go into my garden because of the toil and sweat, so my garden was neglected, and it showed. The weeds grew tall and no vegetables were to be seen. Now I no longer have a garden, and so I never neglect my garden. Of course, I do not get vegetables, either, but I never neglect my garden. During the years before I owned a car, I never neglected my car, but since I now own one, it happens that from time to time I do neglect my car.

Let us look at the question in Hebrews 2:3: "How shall we escape, if we neglect so great salvation?" In order to learn who "we" are, we turn to chapter 3, the first verse: "Holy brethren, partakers of the heavenly calling." They are the ones who are liable to neglect their salvation. Again note Hebrews 3:12: "Take heed, brethren." These then are "holy brethren, partakers of the heavenly calling." Listen to what is said to them: "How shall we brethren escape, if we neglect so great salvation?"

The Old Testament is valid and operative; its promises are real and they are fulfilled when requirements are met. When the Scripture says: "The word spoken by angels was steadfast, and every transgression and disobedience received a just recompense of reward" (Chap. 2:2) it does not mean so much that the sinner would be criticized and penalized because he did not do what God had asked him to do. The Old Testament is setting

19

forth in its requirements actual, valid promises. The Old Testament promises that if you do the will of God you will be blessed, if you do not obey you will not be blessed. This is a valid, operative principle. Would you expect the word spoken by the Lord Jesus Christ to be less effectual? He was greater than the angels, and if the word spoken by them was true, how much more so would be the word spoken by the Lord?

Look at the words spoken by the Lord Jesus Christ and ask yourself if you think they are valid. Do you think they would work? If the Lord Jesus in this great salvation offers forgiveness, do you think that it would be real? When He says that if you will come to Him, He will take care of you, could you believe it? If you say you trust in Him constantly, will you have assurance? That is what He promises. And if you walk with Him and yield to Him, letting Him work in you, do you think the result will be virtue? That is what He promises.

The writer of Hebrews is saying that you can be absolutely sure. If it is true that when you sin you will be punished, then it is also true that when you follow the will of the Lord Jesus Christ you will be blessed. Yield yourself to Christ Jesus, and forgiveness is yours. Trust in the Lord Jesus Christ, and confidence and assurance are yours. Walk in the ways of the Lord Jesus Christ as led by the Holy Spirit of God, and there will be virtue in your conduct. When you sin, you will be punished; then it is also true that when you follow the will of the Lord Jesus Christ you will be blessed. If you read your Bible you will have faith; if you do not read your Bible, you will not have faith. If you read your Bible, you will come to believe in God. If you read books that criticize the Bible, you will come to doubt God. If you pray to God, you will be blessed; if you do not pray to God, you will not be blessed. That was true in the Old Testament days, and that principle was valid and real; even so the words spoken in the New Testament by the Lord Jesus Christ were valid and real. If you cultivate your garden, you will get beans; if you do not cultivate your garden, you will get weeds. "So great salvation" which was spoken of by the Lord Jesus Christ is this great work of salvation that God will perform when you have Christ, the hope of glory, in you. This is the great blessing which is in Christ Jesus, and this is what He talked about and warned about.

Christ Jesus said that if we turned to Him, we would be blessed; if we neglected to turn to Him there would be no blessing. If we failed to abide in Him, there would be no strength. This truth that salvation is to be found in Him would not be available to anybody not in Him. "I am the door: by me if any man enter in, he shall be saved." "I am the way, the truth, and the life: no man cometh unto the Father, but by me." These promises were valid and real when they were first spoken by our Lord, and He promised salvation in this fashion: "Whosoever cometh to me, I will in no wise cast out," and "Whosoever believeth in me shall not perish but have everlasting life."

This truth was confirmed unto us by those who heard Him. Paul testified everywhere, as did Peter, James and John, that whosoever believed in the Lord Jesus Christ should be saved. What the apostles preached was actually true because of the evidence in the lives of the people who believed. " . . . God also bearing them witness, both with signs and wonders, and with divers miracles, and gifts of the Holy Ghost, according to his own will?"

So we could say with the writer of Hebrews that in view of the actual results of following the Lord Jesus Christ, who could reasonably be indifferent to the challenge of the gospel? How can we escape if we neglect so great a salvation? We have the Bible and if we do not read it, do you think we are going to escape the fact that we will lack faith?

Chapter 4

THE SON OF GOD CAME TO SUFFER

Thou madest him a little lower than the angels; thou crownedst him
with glory and honor, and didst set him over the works of thy hands
(Heb. 2:7).

The latter part of Hebrews 2 continues to focus upon the Lord Jesus
Christ whom God used to bring the revelation of the new covenant into
this world. The Scripture we have in Hebrews 2:4-10 presents two truths
that are in contrast to each other. We learn that God gave Christ great
power. God gave Him power over all, and at the same time the Son of
God came in a lowly state. Human beings would not seem to rate as fit to
associate with God, and it is astonishing that God would send His Son to
be made like a man, because man can die and God cannot die. Yet God
put the Son of Man in control over everything. The limitations of man are
such that in the course of nature he will die. But God has arranged to
secure his prestige. The greatness of man is promised. He is to have
dominion over all.

Everything said about the significance of man in the plan of God was in
a sense personified and manifested in Jesus of Nazareth. He was born into
the world in the form of a man and was made mortal in the sense that He
could and would die, yet He was always in Himself the Son of God. The
marvelous truth is that the Son of God is actually involved in death itself.
In verse 9 we read: "But we see Jesus, who was made a little lower than
the angels for the suffering of death." Angels do not die and had the Lord
Jesus Christ been made in the form of an angel He would not have died,
but He was made in the form of man in order to die. The birth of Jesus of
Nazareth was not the case of a child born in this world by the will of the
flesh. The Son of God came into this world as He did because His Father
willed it to happen in this way. He took on the nature of Abraham, coming
into this world that He might die, in order that He might fully demonstrate
what was involved in living the will of God in this world.

Because Christ Jesus lived and died and rose from the dead, He opened the way for us to come unto Him. The record is that Jesus of Nazareth was purposely made a little lower than the angels so that He could suffer death. But we see Him "crowned with glory and honor," which refers to all that the prophets said would happen to Him. While He lived as Jesus of Nazareth the glory and honor were not seen. Only on the Mount of Transfiguration was the glory shown for a moment. But the promise is that the day will come when all glory and power and might and dominion will be given to the Lamb who sits on the throne — the Lamb that was slain and is alive forevermore, and all heaven will praise Him. He will be crowned with glory and honor because, by the grace of God, He tasted death for every man. It was not that He was crowned with glory and honor that He might taste death for every man, but He was made a little lower than the angels for the suffering of death, that He might taste death for each of us.

> For it became him, for whom are all things, and by whom are all things, in bringing many sons unto glory, to make the captain of their salvation perfect through sufferings (Heb. 2:10).

This is a marvelous statement. It seemed to be proper, so far as God's overall plan was concerned, that the Son of God, who was actually the Creator and the keeper and the provider, "for whom are all things, and by whom are all things," should bring many sons unto glory. When Jesus Christ came to work it out to save many people, it was appropriate that God should "make the Captain of their salvation perfect through sufferings." This word "perfect" means mature, full grown. He was to enter into the fullness of His stature because of the things He suffered.

I suspect everyone knows that suffering is the common lot of men, and no one lives very long until it is realized in one way or another. Now suffering can work out to a person's benefit, but this is not always the case. The evidence is that there are people who become sour or bitter through suffering. They want nothing to do with God. But there are others who, when they suffer, look up to God and trust in Him. The Lord Jesus did not have anything to be set free from, but He suffered in order that He might grow into fullness and fully understand what is involved when in weakness you die and put your trust in God. There is suffering of all kinds and some of it is grievous. There are people who live day in and day out constantly in suffering. It would be difficult for them to understand that this suffering can actually work for good for them, but it is true. One needs a spiritual frame of mind and understanding to grasp that.

A great many people have difficulty seeing how a person who is in trouble is being blessed, but this is the truth of the gospel. It happened to the Lord Jesus Christ, although He was the Captain of their salvation, the leading one in the salvation program. He was made perfect, mature. What this word "perfect" means is somewhat like this: "If you have apples in the orchard you will know in the spring the tree is covered with blossoms. Each blossom is potential fruit, but there will not be that many apples on the tree, because some of the flowers will fall off. After the apples begin to grow it can be noted they do not ripen at once. There will be little green apples which get bigger and bigger until they are ready to eat. The word *maturing* means "growing into the fullness of stature."

From a spiritual point of view this growth takes place as one suffers. I am reiterating this because I think it is very important to keep in mind that the Lord Jesus Christ (even though He was God) in order that He might adequately help us, came into this world and suffered so that He would know what was actually involved. When we say He was made perfect through suffering we do not infer that He had been imperfect before, in the sense there was fault in Him. He was imperfect in the way a growing child is not yet a perfect man, in the way a young apple tree that does not have apples on it is not yet a full fledged, mature apple tree. There may be nothing wrong with that apple tree at a year old but it will be some time before that tree can bear fruit because it is not mature. That is the way it is with believers. The child of God needs to grow in grace and he can do this by following Him who came into this world to learn what was necessary in order to bring us to God.

Chapter 5

CHRIST JESUS, THE DELIVERER

Do you realize that everything that happened to Jesus Christ was planned to help in the saving of souls?

At this point the work of Christ as deliverer is stressed and this is what we see in these words:

> For both he that sanctifieth and they who are sanctified are all of one: for which cause he is not ashamed to call them brethren (Heb. 2:11).

There follow several verses in which the believers are called brethren. As we look into this we see that both He who sanctifies and they who are sanctified are all of one. In what sense would they be all of one unless it would be this? Just as Jesus of Nazareth was begotten of Mary by the power and the grace of God, through the Holy Spirit, so the person who becomes a believer is born again by the grace of God coming into his heart.

In the course of the history of the Lord Jesus Christ, He had no human father and in the course of the history of the individual soul there is no human parent. The individual believer is a child of God, begotten of God through His Word which is made alive in the heart of the believer through the Holy Spirit. Jesus of Nazareth, as He was born of Mary, was not the child of Joseph; He was actually the child of God. Because this was so, He was born by the power of God; even so believers are born by the power of God. He had life because the grace of God was given to Mary, and believers have life because the grace of God is given to them in their hearts. For this reason He is not ashamed to call these believers brethren, because they have one Father.

> I will declare thy name unto my brethren, in the midst of the church will I sing praise unto thee (Heb. 2:12).

Thus it appears He calls the members of the church His brethren.

And again, Behold I and the children which God hath given me (Heb. 2:13).

Here the Lord Jesus Christ sees Himself before God as who He is and sees the believers as being God's children, begotten as it were by the power of God. In this Scripture the Lord stresses the relationship between Himself and the believers. He counts them as His brethren and is not ashamed to do so because they come from the same source. They are alike begotten of God and in this aspect both Christ and the believer are of God.

In Hebrews 2:14-15 we learn that the incarnation (Christ's becoming flesh) was part of a total tactic. This was His way of doing — His maneuver, His procedure — by which He managed to get people saved. At this point the fact is stated that He became flesh to save us out of the flesh. He came down into the human situation so that He might deliver men out of their situation into His own. This coming in the flesh was the way in which He could help human beings. It is very much like a swimmer who sees someone drowning. Let us say that an accident occurs and a boy is in danger of drowning. Among those standing by is someone who can swim. The way that person can get the boy out of the water is not by calling out instructions to the boy. He does not at long distance try to guide the boy to a place where the boy will be safe. What he does is dive into the water to save the boy. So the Lord Jesus Christ came into this world as man, in order that He might save us who have sinned in the sight of God. He took upon Himself the form of man, limiting Himself to human nature and living as a man, in order that He might save us.

> Forasmuch then as the children are partakers of flesh and blood, he also himself likewise took part of the same; that through death he might destroy him that had the power of death, that is, the devil; and deliver them who through fear of death were all their lifetime subject to bondage (Heb. 2:14-15).

The Lord Jesus Christ died as He did in order to destroy the power of Satan. Satan would be involved in putting Him to death, but God raised Him from the dead and that foiled the purpose of Satan. Christ Jesus was not disturbed about the prospect that Satan would oppose Him, because He could overcome him by dying under Satan's hand and being raised from the dead by the power of God. The Lord Jesus Christ won this victory over Satan by yielding Himself to the total situation, and being put to death. When He arose from the grave He opened the way for others to follow, and in so doing, even though He died for us, He was also raised for us. In this way He was able to gain the victory over death so that we, too, can be spared.

Christ Jesus came purposely and the incarnation, His taking on human form, was on purpose.

> For verily he took not on him the nature of angels; but he took on him the seed of Abraham. Wherefore in all things it behooved him to be made like unto his brethren, that he might be a merciful and faithful high priest in things pertaining to God, to make reconciliation for the sins of the people. For in that he himself hath suffered being tempted, he is able to succor them that are tempted (Heb. 2:16-18).

The Lord Jesus Christ learned how it was to live in this world under the rule of God, and so anyone believing in Him is helped to live in this world and to be raised from the dead by the power of God.

Chapter 6

CHRIST IS BETTER THAN MOSES

If you want to help a person get right with God can you think what would be better than to tell him what to do?

> Wherefore, holy brethren, partakers of the heavenly calling, consider the Apostle and High Priest of our profession, Christ Jesus; who was faithful to him that appointed him, as also Moses was faithful in all his house (Heb. 3:1-2).

The writer of this epistle is now focusing our attention on the person of the Lord Jesus Christ. The New Testament epistles were written to help us understand more about the gospel. A believer can grow in grace and in knowledge. He can come closer and closer to God in spite of the fact that he may have already committed himself to Him. The book of Hebrews is written in the New Testament to help believers have the new and greater benefits that are possible in Christ Jesus. Our present study is in chapter 3 where the Lord Jesus is presented as better than Moses. When we use the word "better" we are not so much comparing these two servants of God in themselves. We are not speaking of the fact that one is more honest than the other, nor that one is kinder than the other. We are thinking about their function — that this one with His work is more significant than that one with his work.

Consider the building of a church. In order to build a church it would be necessary first to have a building lot. Then there would be an architect's plan. As important as that architect's plan is, I believe you will agree that the materials — the steel girders, brick and stone and other materials that go into this building — are better than the architect's plan.

Think about someone in your family who has been absent for a length of time in military service. If that person came home on furlough, can you see that the soldier sitting in your home is better than any picture of him? So it is with reference to the things of the gospel. The Old Testament pointed us forward and told us about the Lord, but the New Testament actually presented Him.

In Scripture God reveals what He wants men to do and what He will do. He first reveals that, and then God does what He says He will do. This is included in His work. Moses shows us what God requires and that is very important. Christ Jesus does what God requires and that is even more important. If you wanted to build a fire in the fireplace, you would first bring in the wood and place it in the fireplace. Next you would bring the match which would actually light it. These are two different acts. Actually getting the fire started is more important than placing the wood at the beginning.

What is the whole Bible about? Isn't it about bringing a sinner into the will of the living God? Christ will save the sinner, and Christ will also bring him to joy and blessedness in the will of God. Moses had something to do with this and Christ Jesus has something to do with this. Moses revealed the law of God; Christ Jesus revealed the grace of God. These are not two ways of doing the same thing, but are actually two phases of one purpose that needs to be accomplished. It is important to teach the law as Moses did, and having taught the law and brought before the people the fact that this is what God requires, Christ Jesus then reveals the grace and plan of God.

In an operation of any kind there is a beginning and an ending. The beginning is essential; without the beginning there would not be anything. But the ending is also essential. Without the ending everything done would be to no avail. So in Christian experience, it starts with receiving the Lord Jesus Christ as Savior and where it ends is by walking with Him as Lord and yielding to Him in daily life. Between the beginning and the end — between the starting of the Christian life and mature living with Christ Jesus — there are many casualties. Many do not make it. In writing to the Galatians, Paul said: "You did run well; who did hinder you?"

Again, an illustration from everyday life: In baseball getting to first base is essential, but that does not mean a run has been scored. Getting to first base is necessary; if a player did not get there he would never get anywhere. But from first he must go to second base, and that is important. From second he must go to third, and that is important. However, all that he did before will not help him unless he goes on to home and scores. Now the book of Hebrews focuses attention upon this part; it is written to make sure that you get around to home plate.

> But Christ as a son over his own house; whose house are we, if we hold fast the confidence and the rejoicing of the hope firm unto the end (Heb. 3:6).

"Holding fast unto the end" is the whole substance of this book. Do not quit. You have made a good start in Christ Jesus. Keep it up. Go on through until you are completely where God wants you to be. We read in this portion how Moses was faithful, but how Christ Jesus was more important than Moses.

> Who was faithful to him that appointed him, as also Moses was faithful in all his house. For this man was counted worthy of more glory than Moses, inasmuch as he who hath builded the house hath more honor than the house. For every house is builded by some man; but he that built all things is God. And Moses verily was faithful in all his house, as a servant, for a testimony of those things which were to be spoken after; but Christ as a son over his own house; whose house are we, if we hold fast the confidence and the rejoicing of the hope firm unto the end (Heb. 3:2-6).

To know the right things in the sight of God as Moses would teach you in the Ten Commandments is good, but yielding yourself into the will of God and letting the Lord Jesus Christ work through you to accomplish these things is better.

It is a fine thing to have the architect's plan, but it is much better to have the materials on the ground and the workmen actually working to develop the plans.

Chapter 7

UNBELIEF PROVOKES GOD

Can you imagine how anything would ever provoke God?

Take heed, brethren, lest there be in any of you an evil heart of
unbelief, in departing from the living God (Heb. 3:12).

The Scriptures are full of assurance of the loving kindness of God. In
reading the Scriptures we become more and more convinced of His
long-suffering and His patience, and we marvel at times at His meekness
and what seems to be humility. How easily He comes to any of us,
regardless of who we are, and how gracious and generous He is in His
loving kindness. However, we must not drift into error in this matter.
Though tender, God is not soft; though gentle, He is not weak. We could
have expected there would be something strong about God from such
passages as this: "He resisteth the proud and giveth grace to the humble."

In the earthly life of our Lord there were instances that to some people
would seem strange and out of character. We need in our thinking of the
Lord Jesus Christ to remember there was a time when He came into the
temple, and seeing the money-changers and those who were in the temple
selling doves and cattle, He made a whip and drove them out, saying,
"Make not my house a house of merchandise." This was the Lord and we
get the impression of stern action. Again there is His message to the
church at Laodicea, when He told them He wished they were hot or cold,
but because they were neither hot nor cold but lukewarm, He would spew
them out of His mouth. There are no words of contempt so graphic as
these used by our Lord Jesus Christ.

We should also remember His long denunciation of the scribes and
Pharisees in Matthew 23, when He openly and bluntly declared before the
whole world they would not escape a definite judgment of God because of
their conduct. On another occasion He gave warning to any who would

harm one of His little ones, saying: "It would be better for that man if he had never been born or if a stone had been put around his neck and he would have been put in the depths of the sea." All of these instances in the life of the Lord Jesus Christ might seem to some to be out of character, but they actually belong to the truth. "God is not mocked."

In this epistle to the Hebrews written to believers we have a stern reminder that since God is a rewarder of those who diligently seek Him, these holy brethren, partakers of the heavenly calling, are urged to avoid the peril of provoking God. Provoking God does not occur because a person is weak or ignorant. It occurs when a person fails to respond under conditions when he might have known what to do or he could have known what to do.

We can learn much from this incident which we call "the great provocation" as it is described in Hebrews 3:7-11. This incident occurred at Kadesh-Barnea when the children of Israel had been challenged to go on in and possess the land. They had sent spies ahead. The spies had come back to report it was a good land, but there were high walled cities and the soldiers were giants. Although Joshua and Caleb (two of the spies) urged them to go forward because God would be with them and help them, the people did not go because they were afraid. They did not believe God would help them against those high walled cities and those giants. This was provoking to God because these were the people who had seen the plagues in Egypt. They knew what God could do. They had experienced the passover; and they had passed through that graphic experience of the Red Sea, when God had opened the waters so they could pass through, and then had let the waters return when Pharaoh had tried to pass through with his men.

These were the people who, when they reached the desert (a country where they had not been before), were guided in the day by the pillar of cloud and at night by the pillar of fire. These were the people who when they were beset by an enemy called Amaleck were victorious; Moses fervent praying on the mount gave Joshua the victory. These were the people who had gathered around Mt. Sinai and there had received the Law of God, the Ten Words of Moses. They had received instructions about the tabernacle and the sacrifices and the priesthood, and they had been given to understand how they could order themselves in their travels. They had set up the tabernacle; they had brought their sacrifices, and the priest had assured them that God had forgiven their sins. These were people who had been kept by the faithfulness of God. Although they had passed through experiences in which they had disobeyed God, He had chastened them and brought them back to Himself.

Yet these people, with all these experiences they had in two years of traveling through the strange land, had no confidence in Him at this time. They failed to obey because they did not believe in His power, and this is what provoked God. This is very sobering to us. We may make a decision not to do something God wants us to do because we are afraid that He cannot take care of us. We should be very careful about such because this is what can provoke Him. When He was provoked: "He sware that they should not enter into His rest." He announced that this generation would never realize the fullness of God. This is a sobering thought and a warning to us; it points out the way believers can lose blessing by failing to keep trusting God and to be obedient.

> Take heed, brethren, lest there be in any of you an evil heart of unbelief, in departing from the living God (Heb. 3:12).

"Take heed — be alert" means to keep your conduct under critical eye. Watch yourself lest there be in you a heart of unbelief. Unbelief is not quite like doubt; it is failure to obey by departing from the living God when the believer is called to obey. The believer departs from the living God when he does not go when God asks him to go, or when he does not do what God asks him to do.

It is like a little boy going with his mother to the store. She wants him to keep up with her; he wants to stop and look at toys. In doing this he gets lost. All he did was to stand still; yet what actually happened was that he departed from his mother. Let us not forsake God in this fashion.

Chapter 8

THE IMPORTANCE OF TODAY

Do you realize that if you are ever to get anything done you will have to do it today?

But exhort one another daily, while it is called today (Heb. 3:13).

The writer of this epistle is urging his readers to be sure to get the full blessing of God. He urges them to obey God all the way, that they might have the fullness of the blessing. You have heard that old saying: "There is no time like the present." Some time ago it was my privilege to teach Bible to our missionaries in Mexico at their annual meeting. I met some of the Mexican-Christians, and one man was particularly interesting to me. He was a doctor who was resigning his practice that he might devote himself to leading his church in what we would call home-mission work. He was interested in new work in churches, especially in rural communities and throughout the whole country of Mexico, while the gospel was being taken by Protestant missionaries all over the country. This doctor talked with me about my teaching and preaching, and said he would be glad if some of this material could be put on tape recordings so that his pastors could have it in Spanish. I told him that soon I hoped it could be done. He answered: "Don't say soon. 'Today' is the Holy Spirit's day. That is the only day mentioned in the Bible." "Today if ye will hear his voice, harden not your hearts" (Heb. 3:15).

The Scripture in chapter 3:13-19 carries this strong note of urgency. "But exhort one another daily, while it is called Today; lest any of you be hardened through the deceitfulness of sin." Have you ever stopped to think about that word "exhort"? It will help to understand something about its meaning if I remind you how we ordinarily use it. This is not a word we use in everyday language. We would not find people on the

34

street talking about exhorting one another. But we would see what is meant at every football game and often at basketball games, because the outstanding American illustration of an exhorter is a college or high school cheerleader who leads the entire student body in exhorting the players to win.

Some years ago in the Methodist Church there was a class of preachers who were ordained to be "exhorters." Perhaps these were men who did not have much education but they did have religion. When these men preached it was not that they said anything new, but they repeated things that have been heard before, and they put great emphasis upon them. Much of their message was repetitious. As tedious as that preaching may have been, there were some who got the idea they should get right with God. Human beings are like that; they may need to be told over and over to do the very thing they know should be done. This is what an exhorter does.

I remember something like being exhorted in my own life. It was not a person; it was a mechanical contrivance about which I still have all kinds of feelings, and most of them are dislikes. It was an alarm clock. I can tell you that as a young man I thought an alarm clock was the worst thing man's ingenuity had invented. All it does is urge you to get up out of bed. And when are you to get up? When it rings — now! Of course, you know how anybody feels about that. That is what these exhorters were: They urged one another right now to do immediately the very thing they wanted to do.

"Exhort one another daily"; this responsibility belongs to all of us. I should help you and you should help me, and we should help the other person. We should all be telling each other over and over again to do it NOW — the only time you can do anything. Have you ever thought about that? Any time you ever do anything, you do it today. You cannot do anything tomorrow — you are not there yet. You cannot do anything yesterday — you are past that.

"Lest any of you be hardened" does not necessarily mean that you will become callous to judgment of sin or anything like that, but one may become hardened to the voice of the Holy Spirit. You may delay getting up until that alarm clock runs out; then you just don't get up, because you have become hardened to the sound of it. "Lest any of you be hardened through the deceitfulness of sin." One might ask how sin is ever deceitful. Sin can be deceitful by saying "This won't count." But it does. Or it may be suggested to you, "It will never matter what you do." But it does matter what you do. Or you may think you will have another chance; yet you may not. Sin may easily deceive you into thinking another time is just as good. But another time will never come; it is now that counts.

For we are made partakers of Christ, if we hold the beginning of our confidence steadfast unto the end (Heb. 3:14).

When believers are made partakers of Christ they actually share in His life; He is in them and they are in Him. The beginning of their confidence is the kind of faith they had when they were converted and they began to serve the Lord. If they keep that steadfast unto the end, they will enter into the things of Christ. They should remember when they started to follow the Lord, because now is the time to keep it up all the way through life. The faith that was exercised when they accepted Christ is the same kind of faith that will lead into consecration and full time service.

In verse 16 it is revealed that some people who started never arrived. "For some, when they had heard, did provoke." There are some people who provoke God. Such might be in our own family or among our friends. We should be very careful about who influences us, because some people do provoke God. These stopped walking with Him. "But with whom was he grieved forty years? was it not with them that had sinned, whose carcases fell in the wilderness?" Those who did not go on grieved Him. "And to whom sware he that they should not enter into his rest, but to them that believed not?" These people did not obey Him; they did not go forward when He asked them to, and they were the ones with whom He was provoked. They could not enter in because of unbelief.

The real reason for their being provoking to God was not their weakness, nor even their sin, as much as it was their failure to obey. They put no confidence in God after all He had done for them.

Chapter 9

BLESSING CAN BE MISSED

Did you know that it is possible to reach a point in Christian experience where you have no need to struggle any more?

The writer urges believing people not to miss the blessing that is available for them, if they will go ahead to do what God wants them to do in the way of yielding to Him. There is perhaps no promise in the gospel so precious as "Come unto me all ye that labor and are heavy laden and I will give you rest." I suspect the statement "I will give you rest" promises the most gracious benefit the human heart can long for, because it is trouble that brings men to Christ for help. When there is strain a person needs Christ to give him grace, and when there is conflict he needs Christ to give him the victory.

This wonderful rest is available, but it must be received. There is such a thing as missing it:

> Let us therefore fear, lest, a promise being left us of entering into his rest, any of you should seem to come short of it (Heb. 4:1).

The great message in this epistle is an exhortation to believing people: They should not miss the blessing available for them. This has happened often in marriage. In any normal situation when a man and woman come together in marriage to live as husband and wife in mutual love, life's richest blessings are available to them. Yet when either fails to attend to certain matters the blessings can be missed. A man may have a lawn with good soil and drainage and good grass, but it must be fertilized and the grass must be cut. If these things are attended to he will have a good lawn; if they are neglected he will not have a good lawn. Doubtless there is much believers do not receive in the way of blessing, not because they are not strong enough or wise enough, but because of their neglect.

How does a person neglect spiritual matters? When he does not obey, when he does not respond when he is called. "The word preached did not

37

profit them, not being mixed with faith in them that heard it.'' Calling did not help those people because they did not come. A mother may call her child to dinner, but the call will not do him any good unless he comes.

The Epistle to the Hebrews aims to exhort believers to act in line with what they know to be the will of God. Whosoever responds to the call of God will find that his days of struggle are over. God will deliver, and God will sustain. Blessing is available to all who believe in Him and are obedient.

Chapter 10

THE NEED FOR OBEDIENCE

If the believer is confident that Jesus Christ paid it all, can you understand how there could be anything left for the believer to do?

> Let us labor therefore to enter into that rest, lest any man fall after the same example of unbelief (Heb. 4:11).

The gospel is glorious in its emphasis upon the free grace of God, and the believer rightly rejoices in the thought that salvation is free, and that God will provide it for whosoever will come to Him. That promise is found throughout the Bible, and there are no conditions attached to it. However, there is an aspect of this whole matter that is emphasized in the Book of Hebrews: This grace of God offered so freely must be received. While it is true that God provides His blessings freely for anybody, it does not follow that everybody gets them. Whosoever comes will be blessed. But let me say again: The man who turns to God must be obedient to the will of God.

This portion of Scripture points out that some miss the full blessing because they do not press on to the conclusion of what they believe. It is as though someone were traveling along on the highway on the right road, but he stopped too soon and never reached the town he was headed for. In baseball a runner may reach third base but no record is kept of that. If he is still on third base when the inning is over, there is no score; he may as well have been called out at first base. The circuit must be completed.

There is a real peril in spiritual matters of stopping short of the full blessing of God. In writing to the Galatians Paul said at one point: "You did run well, who did hinder you?" Some years ago there was the almost incredible incident in a horse race in which a jockey had been ahead to the point where he thought the race was over; when he eased up another horse went ahead and won the race. The jockey lost the race because he stopped too soon. We have in mind there are people who may know what needs to be done; they may know what would be acceptable to God; all of this would be good, yet it could be inadequate. To *do* what we know is better. Moses, in the law, did well to tell the people what to do, but until hearts are changed all that Moses wrote in the law is of no help. So Christ Jesus in grace does better than Moses, because He has the power to change hearts and to bring us into *doing* the will of God. Telling what to do is very important but in itself it is inadequate. The believer needs to go further than that; the heart needs to respond in faith and in obedience to God.

The big problem for me as a human being is that I just do not want to do the will of God. You may show me what there is to receive and I may understand it, but deep down in my heart I want to do my own will. Simply put, here is where the power of the gospel comes in. I may turn myself over to the Lord Jesus Christ and receive Him as my Lord and Savior, but I still can have lurking in me the disposition to be selfish and to be proud of myself. Regardless of how poor my record had been and how weak and wayward I may have been, the moment I come to the Lord Jesus Christ and acknowledge these faults I am received by Him. So I have the joy of fellowship with Him, but right then comes the temptation to feel as though everything is complete. I wanted to become reconciled to God, and now that I am everything is all right. This could be tragic if my response stops here.

When I am reconciled to God, this means He has accepted me and I am now to live with Him. When I yield my soul to Christ as my Savior and receive Him as my Lord, God works in my heart through the Holy Spirit to move me to obedience. This is the source of the joy of the gospel of the Lord Jesus Christ. If I think of the gospel as a set of rules that should be followed, or instruction about certain work I should do and about certain standards I should meet, it will be less than what has been revealed in the New Testament, and it will not work. But if I believe in Him and receive Him as my Savior, trusting the keeping of my soul to Him, God works in my heart something that results in my being born again and gives me a new disposition to want to do the will of God. The Holy Spirit ministers to me, showing me the things of Christ, so that I can walk in them and am blessed. Thus the task of the believer is to seek to enter into this relationship with God. This cannot be done carelessly; I must focus my heart's attention upon the living Lord. I must think about the Lord Jesus Christ being with me at all times and yield myself in obedience to His will. As I yield myself to Him, reading the Bible to learn what He wants me to do, I will be led into the blessing of God.

This is the great possibility for full blessing in Christ Jesus.

Chapter 11

THE BELIEVER CAN COME TO GOD
BECAUSE CHRIST IS HIS ADVOCATE

How can a person be encouraged to come closer to God when he feels his own unworthiness?

> Let us therefore come boldly unto the throne of grace, that we may obtain mercy, and find grace to help in time of need (Heb. 4:16).

The basic admonition in this epistle is an outstanding underlying principle emphasized all the way through as an imperative. The writer admonishes the believer to *go on to the end of his original purpose*. When he started walking with the Lord, what did he have in mind? Did he not intend to be totally yielded to Christ? Now, he should *go ahead and do it!*

This phase of going ahead is really not casual; it is not easily accomplished. There is something about God that fills the soul with awe. As the believer draws near to God he will walk softly in His presence. Doubtless some miss the greater blessing because they feel so fearful at this point that they do not press on. It is possible to feel so fearful one will not come to God at all. It is true of course, that any sincere soul will tremble in the presence of God. God is almighty, holy, just, and good, and He knows all about each person. There are things about any man that are not pleasing in God's sight. Despite this, the believer is to come" . . . boldly unto the throne of grace . . . ."

There is a valid reason why any honest, sincere soul will shrink from coming into the presence of God:

> For the word of God is quick, and powerful, and sharper than any two-edged sword, piercing even to the dividing asunder of soul and spirit, and of the joints and marrow, and is a discerner of the thoughts and intents of the heart (Heb. 4:12).

When we speak of the Word of God we mean more than something written in so many words. The Word of God refers to the mind of God, the whole structure of the thought of God, the judgment of God, and, in a sense, the appraisal of God. This Word of God looking at me and seeing me through and through is evaluating me. "Quick" is an old English term that is difficult for us to understand. It does not mean that God moves rapidly; this word means God is alive. About the only time we use the word in everyday language would be if by chance we should run a sliver of wood under a finger and we might say it went "to the quick." Or if a pin should slip under the fingernail we might say it went to the "quick," viz., the sensitive part of the finger. Anything that produces effect is powerful. That which gets the work done is powerful. Therefore, this Word of God is quick, alive, sensitive, and powerful. It is effectual. It produces results and is "sharper than any two-edged sword."

A sword will penetrate and this Word of God penetrates deep into the heart where it can divide and separate. This is the essence of discrimination — to be able to tell the difference between the good and the bad, the big and the little, the right and the wrong. This Word of God will make one conscious of God Almighty looking down upon us. Therefore we may feel it "piercing even to the dividing asunder of soul and spirit." We mean to say this sharp incision from the Word of God goes down into our hearts. Have you ever heard it said of a certain sermon: "That was a heart-searching message?" This expression would be used when the words of the speaker seemed to enter straight into the heart, and the hearer has the feeling of being inwardly seen, as it were: "even to the dividing asunder of soul and spirit."

No doubt there are many people who are interested in the use of these two words "soul and spirit," but an easy definition is difficult. Sometimes the Bible speaks of a man having body and soul; sometimes it speaks of a man having body and spirit. When these words are used in that way we may have the feeling that "soul" in the one sentence and "spirit" in another mean about the same. *Soul* and *spirit* are often used interchangeably because they are so alike in that they are both immaterial. My opinion is that the word *soul* can refer to one's emotions or feelings, and the word *spirit* can refer to the mind, one's thoughts. This means that the Word of God is so sharp, so penetrating, that it can enter the heart and separate feelings and ideas. "A discerner of the thoughts and intents of the heart" opens up, discerns and sees the innermost thoughts. The result of this is there can be no hiding place from the Lord.

The next sentence brings out this very thought:

> Neither is there any creature that is not manifest in his sight: but all things are naked and opened unto the eyes of him with whom we have to do (Heb. 4:13).

Everything is seen in its true colors; everything is exposed before Him. Perhaps one reason people shrink from coming to God is this fact that is so shattering to personal self-confidence. When I think about coming to God I realize the inner being of my soul will be opened up. I could meet a man and for a time keep my thoughts to myself, but God knows and, because He knows we tremble. There is much about us that should not be and we feel so unworthy in His sight. But the writer goes on not simply to show the believer he should tremble but to give the reason he should have confidence. The believer's hope is in his advocate, a legal term for a lawyer who represents him in court. His case is in good hands. When he is coming before Almighty God, the Lord Jesus Christ is there on his behalf:

> Seeing then that we have a great high priest, that is passed into the heavens, Jesus the Son of God, let us hold fast our profession (Heb. 4:14).

The believer has a representative, an agent. Because this agent is the Son of God, He has access to the throne and He has taken the human frame, the human way of living, right into the presence of God.

> For we have not an high priest which cannot be touched with the feeling of our infirmities; but was in all points tempted like as we are, yet without sin (Heb. 4:15).

The believer's confidence is in Christ because He suffered as men suffer, and because He lived in the flesh in this world so that He knows our plight and can sympathize with us. No wonder the writer can urge so confidently:

> Let us therefore come boldly unto the throne of grace, that we may obtain mercy, and find grace to help in time of need (Heb. 4:16).

The believer is not worthy in himself but Christ is worthy, and the believer's hope is in Christ and his boldness is grounded upon Christ's experience and upon His victory.

A young woman whom I used to talk to was very much burdened because of her past sins. She wanted to know why I was not depressed about mine. I told her the Lord Jesus Christ had carried them away. Because she believed in Him, when I said "trust Him," she found deliverance from that feeling of depression.

Chapter 12

GOD PROVIDES A HIGH PRIEST

Do you know what the Bible means by the word "priest?"

Who can have compassion on the ignorant, and on them that are out of the way; for that he himself also is compassed with infirmity (Heb. 5:2).

This is how a priest is described in the Bible. To be sure, our help is in the Lord and we rejoice in it. We turn to God for our salvation, which is free and is provided through Christ. But let us not draw a wrong conclusion. Sometimes people get the idea that since this is true, everybody is saved. Anybody *can* be saved. But it is seen in the experience of people who have walked with the Lord and have believed in the gospel, that there are several stages to this experience of faith. At any one of these stages the soul may stop short of the blessing available.

When the believer starts walking with the Lord he needs to enter into situations which God has prepared if he really wants the blessings that have been prepared for him. This was pictured in the exodus of Israel. They could not be blessed while they were still in Egypt; so they were told to come out of Egypt. While they were crossing the desert they were to walk in careful obedience. Every day the cloud was over them and every night the pillar of fire guided them. Every morning the manna was on the desert for them to eat; so they were constantly close to the Lord. As they moved through the desert and came to Mt. Sinai, they were instructed in the law and given the truth about the tabernacle and organized for future movements.

Now the Hebrews could not be expected to maintain a perfect record of obedience. God, as revealed on Mt. Sinai, was awesome in His holiness. The people feared Him when they came close and saw the lightning and felt the trembling of that mountain. They were impressed by this outward evidence of His presence. The Hebrews were so sinful there was the danger they would be discouraged. In His grace God provided a helper whom we call "the high priest."

This word "priest" occurs in a group of three words. The Bible tells us how God sent prophets, priests and kings. A prophet is someone who declares the Word of God to the people, telling what God wants done. The priest is someone who would stand for the people in talking with God, someone to enter the presence of God on behalf of the people, praying for them. The king is someone who would control the people to organize them and get something done among them. God provided the high priest who understood how to come to God. He could present the Hebrews as acceptable before God by the shedding of blood. This was a procedure which the priest understood. In this is revealed an amazing aspect of the grace of God. This opens the door to hope for the sinner even now to come into the presence of God. Sin must be taken away, and it *can* be taken away. The wonderful aspect about this is that a person does not have to have a perfect record to come to God. A person can come to God even if his record is not perfect, and his future is not perfect. The priest encourages the sinner to come expecting to be reconciled to God by what the priest knows.

What should the sinner do if he wants to have the blessing of God? He must come into the presence of God to confess his sin that it may be taken away. All of this was known to the priest who knew what to do. In a very real sense he was like a lawyer who appears for his client in court when the client does not know what to do. The wrongdoer needs someone who knows the law who will speak for him. Such a person was the priest who was "ordained of God for men." The Scriptures report plainly this is the function of the priest:

> For every high priest taken from among men is ordained for men in things pertaining to God, that he may offer both gifts and sacrifices for sins (Heb. 5:1).

The priest acknowledges the fact that the man has sinned and he will confess to God that the man has sinned. But he understands about the grace of God, knowing that he can bring sacrifices for the sins, and he does.

> And by reason hereof he ought, as for the people, so also for himself, to offer for sins (Heb. 5:3).

It would have to be that way for every human being, except Jesus Christ. When Aaron and all his sons came into the presence of God, a sacrificial lamb was offered for them. This was a lamb that was offered because no man was worthy to come into the presence of God except the Lord Jesus Christ.

And no man taketh this honor unto himself, but he that is called of God, as was Aaron (Heb. 5:4).

No man became a priest because he studied for it. The priest was given a call from God to function as a priest before Him. Believers should remember now that they are all priests and kings before God. Every believer is supposed to be exercising this function on behalf of other people.

Notice these characteristics of the priest: *the purpose of the priest:* he was ordained for men in matters pertaining to God; *the work of the priest:* he was to offer both gifts and sacrifices for sin; *the manner of the priest:* he was to have compassion on the ignorant. The sinner knew better, but he did wrong; so the priest must have compassion. All of this actually adds up to a great privilege. When the sinner is ignorant he can come to God through the priest — the way that has been opened through the Lord Jesus Christ. The priest's manner is kind and sympathetic, because he knows what the sinner is going through, and is touched by all the feelings of his infirmities. The significance to us today is that God arranged for Christ to be there on our behalf. This is part of His mercy and grace. There is One sent to guide us into the very presence of God. The call goes out to all men: "Come." If a man says: "I don't know what to do," he can find his answer in the Lord, our High Priest. The sinner can come and put his trust in Christ.

Chapter 13

CHRIST JESUS LEARNED OBEDIENCE
THROUGH SUFFERING

Do you realize that it was in order to save men from death that Christ Jesus came into the world to die for sinners?

Though he were a Son, yet learned he obedience by the things which he suffered (Heb. 5:8).

In Hebrews 5:5-10 the truth is set forth about the Lord Jesus Christ's coming into this world. The Son of God came into this world to seek and to save the lost, and to do that He entered into the various experiences that men have here. Perhaps no one will ever fully understand all that was involved when the Son of God became incarnate and came in the form of man. It really amounts to this: When Christ Jesus came into this world to save me, He came into the world as I did, and went through it as I am going through it, in order that He might get me out of where I am. Most of us will not ever fully understand all that this means. In a general way we know that He laid aside His glory. He had been with the Father, perhaps at His right hand, throughout all eternity, and He left that.

We may not fully understand what it meant when He gave up His place of authority, because as the Son of God He would have equal authority with the Father, but He came down to live the life of God in my situation, according to my way of doing things. When He took upon Himself the form of man, He limited Himself to human capacities. Yet if all my salvation depends upon Him, where do I come in? Not only did He come to reconcile me to God that I might be forgiven because He died for me, but He actually came to bring me as a believer into the full blessing of salvation forever. This is what this epistle is discussing. The writer is pointing out that after I become a Christian and am rejoicing in the salvation that is mine because Christ Jesus died for me, I should enter into the fullness of this salvation and allow Christ Jesus working in me to will and do of His good pleasure.

47

"So also Christ glorified not himself to be made an high priest . . . " (Heb. 5:5). This language may be unusual for us, something we would not use ordinarily, yet it has an obvious meaning. Jesus of Nazareth did not exalt Himself. It was not His way of doing things to struggle to make anything of Himself. If I have His Spirit in me and I belong to Him, I will find that I will not be inwardly prompted to exalt myself. God may call me here or there, but I will not seek anything for myself. Christ becomes my High Priest, but God puts Him there.

> . . . but he that said unto him, Thou art my Son, today have I begotten thee. As he saith also in another place, Thou art a priest for ever after the order of Melchizedek (Heb. 5:5-6).

When He came into this world the Lord Jesus Christ humbled Himself to come in the form of man. He emptied Himself of His glory, came into this world as a babe in Bethlehem, and grew up as a boy in this world. He put His whole trust in God. He would be exactly what His Father would make Him to be. His Father made Him to be forever a high priest after the order of Melchizedek.

> Who in the days of his flesh, (and I think this refers to Jesus Christ of Nazareth) when he had offered up prayers and supplications with strong crying and tears unto him that was able to save him from death, and was heard in that he feared (Heb. 5:7).

This seems to be a direct reference to what happened in the garden of Gethsemane. We can learn from this that the Lord Jesus Christ almost died in the garden of Gethsemane. The human frame of the Lord Jesus could barely endure the terrific suffering. His human body was like an electric light bulb through which too large a charge of electricity went. Christ prayed for strength in the garden and received it; that was the only way He could go through with it. The record, "He feared," does not so much mean He was afraid God would do something unexpected or treat Him unfairly, as it does that He appreciated His own weakness and knew His sole dependence was upon the Father. That was how He felt and this is the sense in which this word "fear" is used.

> Though he were a Son, yet learned he obedience by the things which he suffered (Heb. 5:8).

Even in weakness He was the Son of God, but this did not make any difference so far as His actual suffering was concerned. The suffering came in full force on Him, so that He learned what being obedient in this world really means. He found out what dying is by the things which He suffered.

We might think this could be a reason for tribulation on our part. I wonder if we have ever stopped to think that we may need a certain degree of trouble in order to understand what we are saved from, and to appreciate what the salvation of Christ Jesus really is.

> And being made perfect, he became the author of eternal salvation unto all them that obey him (Heb. 5:9).

He was never imperfect at any time. A rose bush is perfect, i.e. complete, when the roses are in bloom. It was growing all spring but was not counted to be really complete until the roses came. Having completed what He came to do, for He came to die for sinners, to be raised from the dead, and to open the way for believers, He was able to save to the uttermost those who would come to God by Him. He became the author of eternal salvation unto all who obey Him. The word "eternal" means it is going on now. It is not just salvation after death, because even now a believer can have it and have it forever.

> Called of God a high priest after the order of Melchizedek (Heb. 5:10).

We shall see that "after the order of Melchizedek" means that He has this office forever and ever, for eternity. It is here that the everlasting quality appears. Because of what the Lord Jesus Christ went through, souls can rest content when they are believers. Christ went through it all, paid the price, knows what it means; and He can produce in believers what is well pleasing in the sight of God.

Chapter 14

MILK IS FOR BABES

Do you realize that as we enter more fully into salvation, new aspects of the truth are more meaningful?

Growing in the grace and knowledge of God is not a matter of years as it is in the physical life, the ordinary life that we know. When we say a child is four years old we know what to expect. If the little girl is eight and the boy is twelve years old, the years spell out just what we can expect. But this is not true spiritually speaking. If a person were to say that he had been a believer for sixteen years, you would not know for sure whether that person is nearly mature or if he has been mature for years. There is a definite period when we first become believers, when as babes we need milk insofar as doctrine is concerned. This milk is not inferior in significance, but it is such aspects of the truth as are suited to a child's mind. It is surprising the things a child's mind should have.

Hebrews 5:11-14 tells about the different stages of maturity and how meaningful they are. "Of whom we have many things to say, and hard to be uttered, seeing ye are dull of hearing," refers to Melchizedek, about whom we shall discuss later. What would be the significance of "hard to be uttered"? A common way of saying that would be "hard to put into words." Why? Because we who listen do not know the words. It would be like going to a mechanic who has investigated what is wrong with the carburetor of your car. He knows the names of all the parts; so you ask him what is wrong with it. He could tell you the names of the parts that are out of order, but you might not know what he was talking about. If you went to a doctor for a physical examination, and he reached the conclusion there was something about your body that was not as it should be, any attempt to describe that to you by using medical terms might not be understood. About such terms you could say "They are hard to be uttered," because in using such terms the fact is "you are dull of hearing."

Some of us enjoy music although we may not fully appreciate the delicate differences in music by the masters. The same may hold true about art; so in these matters we may be "dull of hearing." And so, with reference to spiritual matters, a person may be "dull of hearing." Some years ago I overheard several Korean students talking in their native language; I could not understand one thing they were saying. I was "dull of hearing." The writer here is saying he would like to tell us a great many things about the Lord Jesus Christ being made a priest after the order of Melchizedek, but they are hard to put into words because we do not know the words.

> For when for the time ye ought to be teachers, ye have need that one teach you again which be the first principles of the oracles of God; and are become such as have need of milk, and not of strong meat (Heb. 5:12).

He is saying they have been believers long enough to understand the truth. By now they should be teachers. The oracles of God are the Scriptures. The "first principles of the oracles of God" means the ABC's of the Bible. Do you have need that one should teach you again the ABC's of Scripture? In that case you have become in need of milk and not of strong meat.

The writer points out that everyone who uses milk is a babe but strong meat belongs to those who are of full age: "For every one that useth milk is unskillful in the word of righteousness; for he is a babe." How can one be skillful in the word of righteousness? The skillful person is one who understands the meaning of the passages. It could be that you believed the truth at first and you have believed the truth since then. It could be that you believe the truth now, but if you would learn more about the truth it would become richer to you. All that you believed would still be true, but it would mean far more than it ever has before. A person may say: "I just believe in following the Lord." That is a good general statement, and you and I could understand it right away. But do you realize that means you are not going out of the house without Him? Do you realize that when you drive your car, you are driving in the presence of the Lord; and when you go to shop you are actually walking along with the Lord? He is urging you to follow Him. You will not be trying to make something big of yourself. You will want to serve Him that He might be glorified, because then you will be blessed. As a mature believer you would readily understand this.

Chapter 15

THE MAJOR PRINCIPLES OF THE GOSPEL ARE THE MILK

Have you any idea of the kind of truth that would benefit young believers?

> Therefore leaving the principles of the doctrine of Christ, let us go on unto perfection; not laying again the foundation of repentance from dead works, and of faith toward God (Heb. 6:1).

We have been noticing in this book of Hebrews there is recognition of the fact that in spiritual experience a person following the Lord begins as a babe in Christ. Then as he feeds on the Word of God he grows more and more into the fullness of stature, becoming a mature person. In this way he follows normal growth. When we preach to unbelievers (and that is what we do when we face the world and are conscious constantly of the fact that there will be people who do not yet belong to God through faith) we stress the call of the Lord: "Come unto me and be ye saved all you ends of the earth." When anyone comes we rejoice, because now we have another sinner who repents. And we know there is joy of the angels in the presence of God over one sinner who repents.

This particular aspect of the experience would not be so noticeable when the person who comes is a child who has been born into a Christian home, because there may not seem to be any great change in such a person who has been trained in the ways of the Lord. When this child comes to faith he keeps on in the way he has been going. It is more obvious, however, when the person who is accepting Christ is an older person. Even so many tend to feel that with the acceptance of the Lord all is finished. We are inclined at this point to celebrate and to conclude that everything that should have been done has been done. It is true that something important has happened, a very important matter has been settled. A real event has occurred when a person comes to faith in the Lord Jesus Christ. The matter of accepting Him as Savior is very meaningful. It is a time for rejoicing. But in the Scriptures we read that as newborn babes, believers should desire the sincere milk of the Word that they may grow thereby.

Let us consider now what is meant by this phrase, "sincere milk of the word." If a babe is to grow, what kind of truth would help? The clearest summary of this truth in the New Testament is in this epistle.

> Therefore leaving the principles of the doctrine of Christ, let us go on unto perfection; not laying again the foundation of repentance from dead works, and of faith toward God, of the doctrine of baptisms, and of laying on of hands, and of resurrection of the dead, and of eternal judgment. And this will we do, if God permit (Heb. 6:1-3).

We must go on to maturity, to completeness. Some truth had been known to them as beginners, but as they grow, they must go on to other things.

"The foundation of repentance from dead works" is the first thing mentioned. The sinner must give up on himself. He must acknowledge his sinfulness and feel that everything he does is like a dead thing before God. So he repents — he turns away from and judges as unworthy the works which he had personally done. This is the first aspect of a believer's experience, and to reach this and preach this is a basic foundation truth.

"Faith toward God" is the second step. Faith is a common word, but note that here it is faith toward God that counts. This kind of faith is vital. The believer must turn away from his own dead works as unworthy and receive in his heart the Lord Jesus Christ who is worthy.

The "doctrine of baptisms" probably refers to washings, cleansings. In the ritual of worship followed in the tabernacle when a worshiper was coming to God, the first thing he came to was the altar, where the sin offering was slain and the blood was sprinkled over the tabernacle in his behalf. From there he moved to the laver where there was water for washing. At the altar where the sin offering was offered the worshiper confessed his sins on the head of the lamb which was slain. The important truth there was that he confessed his sin. The second article of furniture was the laver where the man who had confessed his sin was washed; so at this point there was cleansing.

I believe the "laying on of hands" has to do with the giving of responsibility for special service and leadership. The idea that he is given a work to perform would come very soon to a believer. Some commission is given to him about which he is to be obedient in days to come.

The "resurrection of the dead" is a very important truth that is told at the very beginning to believers. The resurrection of the dead emphasizes the reality of eternal life, and the fact that this life here, which ends in death, is by no means all. There is another life that goes on after death into everlasting life. This is a matter of setting heaven over against earth, and the spirit over against the flesh. This was taught to young believers.

Finally, the truth "of eternal judgment" — the reality of ultimate destiny of either heaven or hell, must be taught at the very outset of the life of faith. Even little children can grasp the significance of the final outcome in the living process.

Each of these truths is important, for is not this summary the whole content of the gospel? In a sense it is. These are ultimate considerations, the final stages of faith. The question is: Should these be taught to beginners? Certainly! This will enable people to know where they are going. The meaning is always clearer when the end results are pointed out. We formulate our ideas in terms of what they will mean ultimately. For instance, if a boy and girl are keeping company with each other, that is very interesting, but what really gives this meaning is the fact that they could get married. A man accepts Christ and he wants to be saved all the way. He may not know everything about it, but right now he can learn that ultimately and eternally there will be those who go to heaven and there will be those who will go to hell. He does not want to go to hell. He wants to go to heaven, so he accepts the Lord Jesus Christ. He understands that he can get help from God; so he turns to God for that help. He understands he has sinned and this sin needs to be washed away. He believes in the washing away and in the cleansing of sin.

All these truths the beginner would receive as the milk of the gospel.

Chapter 16

PERSISTENT OBEDIENCE AS LED BY THE SPIRIT PRODUCES RESULTS

Do you realize that many persons who start believing in Christ Jesus fall away from obedience and so miss the glory of the promises of God?

> But, beloved, we are persuaded better things of you, and things that accompany salvation, though we thus speak (Heb. 6:9).

This study will take us into one of the most difficult passages of the New Testament. Many sincere people have quite different interpretations of what these verses mean. I shall give my interpretation very humbly, not necessarily intimating that others are wrong, but pointing out what I believe to be true. As we approach this portion remember that in this book of Hebrews until now the Old Testament incident that has been greatly emphasized has been the experience of Israel at Kadesh-Barnea, the spot in the desert where they failed to go forward because of unbelief when they had the opportunity to go into the land. This has been used as an illustration to warn the people against this peril of not going through to the end of any program after having made a good start.

The writer is stressing going on to perfection — to maturity — emphasizing that we must not falter in obedience and in following the Lord. We should grow in consecration. We can do this by following the guidance of the Holy Spirit of God.

> For it is impossible for those who were once enlightened, and have tasted of the heavenly gift, and were made partakers of the Holy Ghost. And have tasted the good word of God, and the powers of the world to come, if they shall fall away, to renew them again unto repentance; seeing they crucify to themselves the Son of God afresh, and put him to an open shame (Heb. 6:4-6).

Among other things we should immediately take note here of the way things happen when a person turns to God. The believer is enlightened because he really understands the truth. He has tasted of the heavenly gift because he has understood that God will forgive him in Christ Jesus, and he has been graciously blessed in that way by believing this is so. He has had the Holy Spirit work in his heart to show him the things of Christ. He has understood these things better, and, in some cases, for the first time because God has shown him the meaning of them — he has tasted the good Word of God. He has entered into some understanding of Scripture and has seen how it applies in his own life and the powers of the world to come. He has had some intimation of what it is like to be raised from the dead, to have the newness of life, the newness of the Holy Spirit working in him. All of these things follow when a person is a believer.

The writer warns that if believers have real, genuine commencement in walking the way of the Lord; if they should fall away (and this has been the peril recognized throughout this whole book); if they falter and begin to look in the other direction, slacking off in obedience; it would be impossible to renew them again unto repentance. I am inclined to think this is referring to the idea one could not start over as though he had not started at all. When the children of Israel failed at Kadesh-Barnea to go forward and, as a consequence lost the blessing, they were not put back into Egypt. It is true they failed, but they were not returned to Egypt. They were not treated as though they had never started out. When the time came for them to proceed again they did not start with the Passover and crossing of the Red Sea. That was permanently behind them.

It is my belief that when one has heard about Jesus Christ and understands something of the gospel of the Lord Jesus Christ, this is of lasting significance in the soul. There will never be a time in life in the future when he will not remember that. He would have that much in mind in any case. A man might, after several years of marriage, fall into unfaithfulness as a husband. This is very distressing but it can happen. But this does not invalidate the wedding. The fact that he became unfaithful as a husband does not mean that the wedding did not take place, nor does it mean he is no longer married. He does not start over as if nothing had happened. When he wants to live a faithful life again, he does not remarry his wife and start over as if nothing had happened. He needs to return to the duties which he has neglected. He is coming back not as a young man who has never been married before but as a husband who has been unfaithful, and this is different. The backsliding believer, who has in his personal life faltered in obedience to God, is not to be preached to as if he were an unbeliever. That would be treating him as though he had never heard of the Lord, and this would place his previous experience with the Lord in a shameful situation. He *has* heard and because he has heard he is that much more responsible. To treat such a person as an outsider who had never heard the gospel would be to dishonor Christ to whom he once turned, and with whom he had personal dealings.

If I am right in what I have said you will get some inkling of what is involved in the writer's further illustration:

> For the earth which drinketh in the rain that cometh oft upon it, and bringeth forth herbs meet for them by whom it is dressed, receiveth blessing from God: but that which beareth thorns and briers is rejected, and is nigh unto cursing; whose end is to be burned (Heb. 6:7-8).

When the rain comes from heaven it may fall on two pieces of land. One may be good soil, properly prepared, from which is brought forth good grain. The other is not properly prepared; before the rain it was weedy, and thus it was only more weedy after the rain fell. This was not the fault of the rain which made them both grow. The fact they were different was what caused the different results.

The person who for a time followed after the Lord is as a field that instead of bringing forth good grain, brings forth weeds. When that husband neglects his home there will be loss, but he is still married. The cure is not another wedding ceremony, but a humble, contrite attitude on his part. If this erring person receives the things of the Lord Jesus Christ and turns to Him, it will be good. If he receives the Lord Jesus Christ and then falls away and does no more about it, that is bad. But that is not the fault of the grace of God; that is the fault of his own heart. Apparently the emphasis in this portion is on achieving consecration and producing results, with a grave, stern warning of sure loss in case of neglect.

"But, beloved, we are persuaded better things of you, and things that accompany salvation, though we thus speak" (Heb. 6:9). The writer has been discussing the importance of responding obediently to gospel truth and has pointed out the serious results of failure on our part. Any believer who neglects Bible reading, prayer, personal testimony and witness and service will suffer loss. This is the thrust of the book of Hebrews. This book is emphasizing that believers should go on in faithfulness to full consecration.

Chapter 17

PATIENCE IS NEEDFUL

Did you know that a person must respond in his faith diligently if he wants to receive the full blessing that is promised in the gospel?

That ye be not slothful, but followers of them who through faith and patience inherit the promises (Heb. 6:12).

In this particular portion of Scripture the writer is emphasizing to believing people that there are certain conditions under which they can fully obtain the benefits promised of God. Moments of blessing are precious to a believer. The wonderful thing for a believer is to feel about his work in his home or about his daily business that he is acceptable to God and that God is blessing him and looking upon him with favor. The intelligent believer will know that it is not because of anything in himself but because he has yielded to Christ and is trusting in Him.

It is true generally speaking that when a believer puts his trust in the Lord no one can in any way hurt him. You can be absolutely sure of that. We have that promise always. It is also true there are further positive results under God that are real; there are certain results in life that are helpful. Responding to God in the gospel may take the form of exercising ourselves on behalf of others who may be suffering because of preparing themselves to serve the Lord. As the believer seeks to be well pleasing in His sight and responds to His truth, he will find himself becoming interested in others who are in need of help and support.

The Hebrew believers to whom this epistle was written had been warned by the writer earlier in this letter against any lapse on their part to disobedience. He warned them against defaulting from their commitment to walk in service before God. He told them to seek to enter into rest and to be sure to do this despite the tendency to unbelief. The writer now claims he has seen the evidence which would qualify these believers for their blessing. Earlier in this epistle he gave them serious warning that if a person had once known the Lord and then turned away from him, he was not to be treated as a beginner, as a man who did not know better. The fact is he did know better and all would know he was under the judgment of God. If anyone could help him it would be to bring him to God as he is. Yet although he had written that, he now indicates he did not mean to imply that he knew anything about them that would cause him to suspect they might be destroyed. As a matter of fact their record of standing by the men who had preached the disturbing message of the gospel would be known to God. He was sure God would understand their record, and it would bring His blessing. Apparently, however, the full results of God's approval is not to be looked for at once. He will bless now and in the days to come He will bless more.

Even so the full measure of obedience does not occur at one time. Someone may say, "I am really going to obey the Lord." But that is not all done on a Wednesday, but on Thursday, Friday, Saturday, and next week as well, because serving the Lord goes on and on. The blessing from God is the same. The believer does not on any one day have all the blessing he will ever have; there will be more and more. God will increase and continue His blessing as the believer increases and continues his obedience. It was this persistence, this steadfast evidence of actual obedience to God that gave to these Hebrew Christians a quality of excellence that the writer knew about.

> And we desire that every one of you do show the same diligence to the full assurance of hope unto the end (Heb. 6:11).

Keep up what you have been doing! They had been faithful to God in obeying Him, and this obedience had moved them into identifying themselves with other believers, joining those who were seeking to present a gospel testimony to the world. The writer urged every one of them to show the same diligence to the full assurance of hope unto the end. "That ye be not slothful, but followers of them who through faith and patience inherit the promises" (Heb. 6:12).

This emphasizes the fact that the promises of God are not all given at one moment. Believers stand in line for them, as it were. As they continue in faithfulness and obedience, God will continue in His blessing. The richest blessing will come to those who continue indefinitely and completely to do this. The believers are urged not to be slothful. This word takes us into various aspects of literature, but we must not miss what it really tells us. A similar word which is more familiar to us is *lazy*. "Be not lazy." I suspect everyone knows something about that. When a person is lazy he knows what to do but does not do it. There may be another reason but the main problem is that he just does not do it. There is really nothing about the Bible such a person would oppose; in fact, he might defend it. Then why does he not follow the Word? It would take effort. A lazy person just does not want to move. He does not pray now and does not want to start witnessing.

This is a great danger here because something precious could be lost. The writer is urging them not to be slothful but followers of them who through faith and patience inherit the promises. Patience does not particularly have anything to do with longsuffering. It really has a very simple meaning — stick-to-it-iveness! Through patience hang on; stick to it! Sometimes a person may say he has done everything he can. In that case being patient means to hang on and rattle for the rest of the way. Stay with it until the very end. That is patience. Those who really inherit the promises of God are the people who through patience stick to their commitment.

The record in Hebrews 6:13-15 is that Abraham had patiently endured so that he received the promise from God. God promised him that He would bless him so Abraham endured all the way through, on and on, believing the promises. Hebrews 6:16-20 indicates to us the idea that God has given a promise that He will definitely bless those who lay hold on Him. Believers have this "hope as an anchor of the soul, both sure and steadfast, and which entereth into that within the veil." Believers have this promise and if they will continue to trust in God and believe in Him, He will bless them.

Chapter 18

MELCHIZEDEK WAS GREATER THAN AARON

Do you feel that you know what is meant by referring to Christ Jesus as our High Priest?

> For this Melchizedek, king of Salem, priest of the most high God, who met Abraham returning from the slaughter of the kings, and blessed him; to whom also Abraham gave a tenth part of all; first being by interpretation King of righteousness, and after that also King of Salem, which is, King of peace; without father, without mother, without descent, having neither beginning of days, nor end of life; but made like unto the Son of God; abideth a priest continually (Heb. 7:1-3).

This whole epistle focuses attention upon the Lord Jesus Christ and His work, and this is in keeping with the gospel. Believers are being saved by the grace of God in Christ Jesus and everything done for them is by the Lord Jesus Christ. He is the Vine and believers are the branches. He is the Door and believers pass through Him and through no one else. He is the Way, the Truth and the Life, and believers come to God by Him only. There is no other name given under heaven among men whereby believers must be saved. In this epistle He is presented as the eternal High Priest.

Christ Jesus is to be considered as a priest forever after the order of Melchizedek. It is easy to think of a priest as someone who is spoken of as being an officer in a certain denomination. Newspapers will report the activities of certain monks and priests in foreign countries, and the reader may be wondering if the meaning of their function is the same as meant in the epistle. The reader should keep in mind that when the word "priest" is mentioned here in Hebrews, the writer of this epistle has in mind the Bible meaning of the term. The work of Christ as the Son of God is presented in a three-fold fashion: He is spoken of as being prophet, priest and king. Each of these offices means something in the Bible; regardless of what they have come to mean in modern social reference outside the

Bible. When the Bible speaks of a prophet, it is referring to someone who has been chosen as the spokesman for God to the people. The prophet takes the Word of God and says to the people: "Thus saith the Lord." The priest is designated as the spokesman for the people to God; he is the one, who in coming into the presence of God, prays for the people. The king is the one chosen of God to coordinate the activities of the people and to order their affairs relating people to people. Our interest in this study is in the priest as that term is used in the Bible.

What we have learned about the priest is that he is chosen from among the people who understood life the way they lived it. He was to be sympathetic, compassionate, to the weak and ignorant, and to those who were wayward. He was to be intelligent and called of God. No man sought this office for himself. The priest was authorized by God to do his work. In the case of Christ Jesus He was the author of eternal salvation. No man was to come to God except by Him. Although the same word "priest" is used, the writer now indicates the thought that Christ Jesus as priest was superior to Aaron as priest. This is indicated by referring to Him as from the order of Melchizedek of whom the writer of Hebrews says: "Of whom we have many things to say, and hard to be uttered" (Heb. 5:11).

That probably means there will be ideas that are spiritual, not known to men in common, the kind of ideas for which preparation in the Bible is necessary that one may be able to understand what they actually mean. Melchizedek is a double Hebrew word meaning "King of Salem — King of Jerusalem." His function was "priest of the most high God," and he met "Abraham returning from the slaughter of the kings." That was the incident when Abraham delivered Lot from the kings who had captured Sodom, and had taken Lot captive. When Abraham returned, Melchizedek met and blessed him. "To whom Abraham gave a tenth part of all" — the tithe, the portion that was given in the service of God. An ordinary worshiper would give this tithe to the priest as a representative of God.

The name "Melchizedek" has special meaning. "First being by interpretation King of righteousness." When the Scripture says by "interpretation" it means by translation. The word *Melchizedek* is made up of two words: *Melchi* which means "king," and *zedek* which means "righteousness." It means also "King of Salem." *Shalom,* a Hebrew greeting meaning "peace," and *Salem* are the same word; so Melchizedek was King of Salem, which is King of peace.

As far as the record goes Melchizedek had no genealogy. The Israelites did not know whence he came. So far as the record is concerned, there was no birth certificate and no death certificate, so that from a legal point of view it was just as though he had not been born or had not died. He was like the Son of God in that, so far as the record is concerned, he is eternal. Melchizedek appeared; no one knows from where he came or where he went. In that sense he abides a priest continually, which is everlasting. Melchizedek was recognized by Abraham as superior, and their encounter is recorded in verses 4 to 10. Abraham gave him a tithe and received blessing from him. Melchizedek was different from Aaron in that he was a king. We do know that Abraham gave him tithes and received blessing from him. There is also the remarkable idea that Levi, who was a great grandson of Abraham, was considered as being in Abraham when Abraham honored Melchizedek as superior. Levi being in Abraham, his grandfather, shared in this tribute to Melchizedek. We learn from this passage that Melchizedek was greater than Levi and greater than Aaron.

Chapter 19

CONDEMNING THE WRONG
DOES NOT PROMOTE WHAT IS RIGHT

What could possibly be better in a person's spiritual experience than to be forgiven for sin?

The priestly aspect of the work of Christ Jesus is what He does for us when He enters into the very presence of God. He was to be a priest after the order of Melchizedek, who was greater than Aaron. He came to bring superior blessing to be shared with believers. The writer sets forth the idea that Jesus Christ, the great High Priest, is a great person, and now he will show that He does a greater thing than Aaron could ever have done.

> If therefore perfection were by the Levitical priesthood, (for under it the people received the law,) what further need was there that another priest should rise after the order of Melchizedek, and not be called after the order of Aaron? (Heb. 7:11).

An apple tree reaches perfection when apples are on the branches. The apple tree starts as a little seedling, becomes a sapling, grows into a young tree, and it is several years old before the first apples appear. It reaches its prime some years later. The epistle to the Hebrews would refer to this full-fledged apple tree as perfect. It is now complete. In the spiritual sense being perfect or complete is to be full grown, or everything Christ Jesus could make a person to be.

> For the priesthood being changed, there is made of necessity a change also of the law (Heb. 7:12).

When there is a different kind of priest there must be a different kind of operation. There is a real difference in these two orders of the priesthood.

> For he of whom these things are spoken pertaineth to another tribe, of which no man gave attendance at the altar. For it is evident that our Lord sprang out of Judah; of which tribe Moses spake nothing concerning priesthood (Heb. 7:13-14).

Our attention is drawn to the fact that the Son of God, Christ Jesus, was not made after the fashion of Aaron. He did not come from the tribe of Levi; He was made after the fashion of Melchizedek, and actually belonged to the tribe of Judah.

> And it is yet far more evident: for that after the similitude of Melchizedek there ariseth another priest, who is made, not after the law of a carnal commandment, but after the power of an endless life. For he testifieth, Thou art a priest for ever after the order of Melchizedek (Heb. 7:15-17).

The outstanding aspects about Melchizedek were that he was a king, a king of righteousness and of peace, and that he was everlasting. The Lord Jesus Christ as the Son of God was made a priest after the order of Melchizedek; He was greater than Aaron. The writer is arguing just now there must be a law, a condition or a covenant that He works under which must involve a better contract. This is confirmed by what is added: "For there is verily a disannulling of the commandment going before for the weakness and unprofitableness thereof" (Heb. 7:18).

The writer seems to imply that if there is to be a greater priest than Aaron it must mean He is bringing a greater benefit than Aaron. Something about the covenant under Aaron was weak and unprofitable for the believer so something new and different was brought in. "For the law made nothing perfect, but the bringing in of a better hope did; by the which we draw nigh unto God" (Heb. 7:19). When we say the law made nothing perfect, we mean that rules and regulations never brought anybody through to maturity, but the bringing in of a better hope did bring people to maturity.

Here is a truth that is grounded in the nature of man. Disciplining a child by regulations may be necessary and very important, but it will never bring that child through to maturity. Pointing out what is wrong about anything will not promote what is right. Telling a person what is wrong may be very necessary and very important, but it is inadequate. All that is done is to tell the person what was wrong. If he did more of the same, it would be more wrong. But this will not promote that which is right. Stressing that which is good is the way to lead a person away from that which is evil. This is what Christ Jesus does in the covenant of grace which will be seen when the new covenant is studied.

Chapter 20

CHRIST AS HIGH PRIEST
CAN SAVE TO THE UTTERMOST

> Wherefore he is able also to save them to the uttermost that come
> unto God by him, seeing he ever liveth to make intercession for
> them (Heb. 7:25).

This verse is one of the most wonderful in the whole Bible. This epistle
has emphasized repeatedly that Jesus Christ was better than anyone who
had been before Him, and those who were fortunate enough to have the
revelation that came from Jesus Christ would be far better off than any
who had had any previous revelation. Throughout the Old Testament it is
obvious that the revelation of God's will had been presented to His people
again and again, but there was always the same result: It failed to arouse
them to do God's will. God would call them; God would work with them;
God would do for them; yet when the time came for them to obey Him
they would fail.

In former times the truth had been set forth before the people showing
what God would require of them, and this would be done in a plain,
simple way. However, the people did not do it, and one reason was that
they did not have the heart for it. One thing revealed in the Bible over and
over again about man is that he is a sinner. Deep inside the natural man's
heart he is selfish-minded. He wants to promote himself in any way he
possibly can. At any time when any issue comes up in terms of what to do,
he will think of himself. That is natural for the natural man. In Old
Testament times there were hints and promises that one day God would
do differently, but at this point the emphasis is that Jesus Christ was better
than anyone who had gone before.

> For those priests were made without an oath; but this with an oath by
> him that said unto him, The Lord sware and will not repent, Thou art
> a priest for ever, after the order of Melchizedek (Heb. 7:21).

Inasmuch as the Lord Jesus had been made a priest by the oath of God, He
was a better priest than those who had gone before who were made

priests, but not by an oath of God. "By so much was Jesus made a surety of a better testament." He was made a guarantee, a person who would give assurance that there would be better results. That which makes the Lord Jesus Christ a better priest than anyone who went before was the work He came to do, which was more thorough and brought better results because of the very way in which it was done.

> And they truly were many priests, because they were not suffered to continue by reason of death: but this man, because he continueth ever, hath an unchangeable priesthood (Heb. 7:23-24).

Jesus Christ was better than others because they could not continue. Their time of service was short because they would die.

> Wherefore he is able also to save them to the uttermost that come unto God by him, seeing he ever liveth to make intercession for them (Heb. 7:25).

The other priests could not do this. Notice the phrase "He is able to save to the uttermost." Let me suggest that you hold to that word "save." Don't ever let go of it. It has to do with the work of the Lord Jesus Christ. It also has the idea of deliverance and includes the idea of healing. As I have said upon occasion, you can put an *l* in the word *save* and make *salve* out of it. He is able to salve them to the uttermost; He is able to heal. After all, salvation, the noun form of the verb save, has the *l* in it. He is able to save the most needy person — even one whose character has deteriorated extensively. When the Scripture says He is able to save to the uttermost it does not have reference to other people, but to a man's own need; he will be saved. In every respect He is able to save those who come to God by Him. "Seeing he ever liveth to make intercession for them." There will never be a situation about which the Lord Jesus will not be able to intercede. We have a Savior who is pleading in glory, and the keeper of Israel neither slumbers nor sleeps.

This is what makes the work of the Lord Jesus Christ better work than the work of Aaron, who could deal only with those things that the worshiper brought to him. The sinner would come and confess his sins, and Aaron could do something about those sins which had already been committed. He could go into the presence of God, have those sins forgiven, but that was all. Christ Jesus can anticipate; He knows all about me. He can pray for me because "He ever liveth to make intercession" for me, not only when I do wrong, but before I do anything. This is our assurance, that every possible development in our lives is open to God; it is known to Him who is pleading for us.

> For such a high priest became us, who is holy, harmless, undefiled, separate from sinners, and made higher than the heavens; who needeth not daily, as those high priests, to offer up sacrifice, first for his own sins, and then for the people's: for this he did once, when he offered up himself (Heb. 7:26-27).

This is the description by which the Lord Jesus is set forth as definitely superior:

> For the law maketh men high priests which have infirmity; but the word of the oath, which was since the law, maketh the Son, who is consecrated for evermore (Heb. 7:28).

The writer of the book of Hebrews has been stressing that our High Priest can deliver us in every sense and in every capacity.

Chapter 21

CHRIST JESUS CAN DO MORE
THAN AARON COULD DO

Would you understand that when Christ Jesus as our High Priest was said to be better than Aaron, this referred to his work, not his superiority as a person?

The point being made in this epistle is that the work of Jesus of Nazareth was more effectual than the work done by priests in the Old Testament where the demands of the law were set forth as to what God would require of man to be acceptable in His sight. What was effected in Christ Jesus is the inward disposition to want to do the will of God, which goes far beyond what the Old Testament could ever do. This is actually the far better thing believers have today.

> Now of the things which we have spoken this is the sum: We have such a high priest, who is set on the right hand of the throne of the Majesty in the heavens; a minister of the sanctuary, and of the true tabernacle, which the Lord pitched, and not man. For every high priest is ordained to offer gifts and sacrifices: wherefore it is of necessity that this man have somewhat also to offer. For if he were on earth, he should not be a priest, seeing that there are priests that offer gifts according to the law: who serve unto the example and shadow of heavenly things, as Moses was admonished of God when he was about to make the tabernacle: for, See, saith he, that thou make all things according to the pattern showed to thee in the mount. But now hath he obtained a more excellent ministry, by how much also he is the mediator of a better covenant, which was established upon better promises (Heb. 8:1-6).

Believers today have a special kind of priest. In the Old Testament times the priest worked in the tabernacle where he followed the pattern of duties to be performed. Here again let me remind you that what was done in the Old Testament was the revelation of what God requires in obedience. This was set forth in various ways. We were to act toward Him with a reverence to which His position entitled Him. We were to act toward others with consideration because that is the right thing to do, and we were to act toward the poor with charity. In all of this you will find nothing of self. God has never approved of any person being interested in self. It happened however in the Old Testament times that, although the requirements of God were such as have been outlined, man was interested in himself, and did what was pleasing to self. Moses was not able to help the people because they did not want to do what he told them to do, and Aaron was not able to help because he could take care only of the sins already committed; he could not do anything about the nature and disposition of the people who came before him as worshipers.

In Christ Jesus there is one who is better than Moses and Aaron; He is in heaven in the presence of God, whereas the Levites were here on earth in a tabernacle made by man. The real presence of God right now in heaven is created by God Himself. Aaron, even though he was here only in the tent and came into the presence of God in what was a symbol or pattern, offered up sacrifices to God. So the Lord Jesus, who is now in the very presence of God, must also offer something. We shall find that He *does* have something to offer to God: He offers Himself, not only in His death on Calvary's cross, but through His believers.

You will remember that the Scriptures say about God: "He knoweth our frame and remembereth that we are but dust." Then again, He will lead men to Himself with compassion: "Christ died for the ungodly." He will lead men with authority because the Scriptures say about Christ: "Thou art a priest forever after the order of Melchizedek." Aaron, who was an example and who set out a pattern of the eternal things, had his limitations. Despite the fact that he was functioning as God called him to, there were certain things about Aaron that he could not overcome. Aaron was a sinner and had to offer up sacrifices for himself. Also, the sacrifices Aaron brought — the blood of bulls and goats — were inadequate because those sacrifices could not erase sin from the heart of man. While Aaron brought the blood of bulls and goats, Christ Jesus brought His own blood. While the only promise Aaron received from God was that of forgiveness from guilt, Christ Jesus could get from God deliverance from the power of sin. Aaron was temporary and could be a priest for only a little while, but Christ Jesus is eternal, and "he ever liveth to make intercession for them."

In these various ways the writer emphasizes that we have in the presence of God right now on our behalf someone who will do more fully and capably the salvation work of God which Aaron only simulated in the Old Testament. We have something better now in Christ Jesus.

Chapter 22

THE NEW COVENANT

Do you know why there is a New Testament in the Bible?

Behold, the days come, saith the Lord, when I will make a new
covenant with the house of Israel and with the house of Judah (Heb.
8:8).

When considering the Bible as a whole it is a simple thing to remember
that there is an Old Testament and a New Testament. It is easy to think
that the Old Testament is called old because it came first and the New
Testament is new because it came afterwards. There is a sense in which
that is true, but there is a difference in the procedures of the New
Covenant as compared with the Old Covenant, in the New Testament as
compared with the Old Testament. Yet while there is a difference I hope
to show that there is no separation; they are not opposite. They are not two
ways of doing the same thing, although they both do affect the same
person.

Let us look into it closely. If you will remember the story of the Bible as
a whole it is easy to recall that it starts with the creation of man and very
early in the record is the fall of man — the sin in the Garden of Eden. The
dark consequences of sin follow; it eventually ravaged and destroyed
everything so far as man is concerned. Man is doomed. When we think
about this we could wonder why it was ever allowed to happen in that
way. But in that same record also we find that God is a God of grace (Gen.
3:21). In the Scriptures later this becomes even more clear.

For God so loved the world, that he gave his only begotten Son, that
whosoever believeth in him should not perish, but have everlasting
life (John 3:16).

In the course of Bible history we have the story of salvation work as
planned by God. Salvation is not arbitrarily forced on anyone. While it is
true that in creation all men were made, it is not true that all men will be

saved. Only those who respond to the gospel will be saved. The flood came upon all men, but only Noah and his family were saved, because they entered the ark as God had directed. God delivers those who put their trust in Him.

As God's work unfolds there are always two phases. The way the Bible expresses it is: "seedtime and harvest shall not fail." There is a sense in which seedtime is old and harvest is new, but they are not separate. Harvest is not a substitute for seedtime; seedtime has its place and harvest has its place as successor to seedtime. Do not contrast the Old and New Testaments by saying that the Old Testament was all wrong so we start with the New Testament. You may as well say seedtime was all wrong and now we start with harvest. Without seedtime there would be no harvest and this is true insofar as the Bible is concerned. In the process of building a factory there is first the phase of construction; upon completion there is the phase of operation. Each has its place. There were two phases of my army experience: first, I enlisted; after that I served. The enlistment part was in preparation; the service part was in performance.

In the great work of salvation that God is performing in the gospel of the Lord Jesus Christ we should forsake sin and receive eternal life. Sin we have; life we want. The way to deal with sin is to repent; the thing to do with eternal life is to believe in it. Paul talks about the sinful person as the old man. One way to deal with him is to put him off. He talks about the life that is in Christ Jesus as the new man. What to do with Him? Put Him on. We say a man is born in sin — that is his first birth. He can live forever in grace, which is our prospect in Christ Jesus. In dealing with salvation we have these two phases: First, we must deal with sin, and second, we must receive eternal life. For dealing with sin we have the old covenant which operates in the Old Testament. For the receiving of eternal life we have the new covenant which operates in the New Testament. In the Old Testament we have the presentation of the law, and in the New Testament we have the presentation of grace. The two can be contrasted. While grace comes after law, and is far more important and wonderful than law, it is not contrary to law. They work together. Law is the knowledge of sin; grace is deliverance from this sin. It is like dealing with health so far as the doctor is concerned. In diagnosis the doctor decides what is the matter, then the treatment follows which may take a much longer time.

In the relationship between a man and woman there is first courtship, the first relationship; then there is marriage, living with each other forever after. So far as the spiritual experience is concerned, we deal first with self and then we deal with Christ. Dealing with Christ is different from dealing with self, but these belong together. In this way we get the idea that the new covenant will do something more than the old covenant.

Chapter 23

THE GRACE OF GOD PRODUCES GOOD WORKS

Do you understand how the gospel of Christ can be better for a soul than the law of Moses?

I will put my laws into their mind, and write them in their hearts (Heb. 8:10).

One of the sad aspects of human response to God as it is revealed in the Bible has been that man does not want to do that which is good. It is not that he is opposed to the good but he does not want to do what is involved to achieve it. He does not want to do what would be pleasing to God; he wants to do what is pleasing to himself. This leads us to realize how God has arranged matters. When God created man, He made him in such a way that man could live fully and freely if he lived the way God planned for him to live. Such fulfillment of living would follow only when man was obedient to God under His law.

Many times we overlook something that is really obvious in nature. We can see the grass growing, the flowers blooming and the fruit on the trees. We hear the birds sing, and we are conscious of fish in the water. All of these develop and achieve their fulfillment if they live according to the law under which they are made. As far as the grass is concerned, some does not grow; not every flower seed that falls into the ground produces an apple tree. What does this mean? God has created a world in which there are certain conditions under which living can go on. When the conditions are met the flowers bloom, the grass grows, the trees bear fruit, the birds sing and fish are found in the sea. All are subject to the laws of their nature. God has set it up that way.

This is true in nature around us. It is always true. If the conditions are not met the living process is at an end. There is nothing arbitrary in that; it was set up that way, and it is like that in the nature of the whole universe. In the very same way, "the soul that sinneth, it shall die." God has an interest in man that He does not have in flowers, trees, and animals. God so loved man He planned to save him from his mistakes. Man did the very thing that would bring about his death. When man failed to obey God he incurred death just as a plant that does not follow the laws of nature would be counted dead. But God arranged to save man in spite of his having done wrong, although this salvation is not universal. Creation was universal; all things were made, but not all things are saved. This salvation is not coercive and in a certain sense it is provisional: "Whosoever believeth in him shall not perish but have everlasting life." The next clause reads: "Whosoever believeth not is condemned already." The sentence of doom has already been passed.

All men are guilty in the sight of God, but the salvation program is to save man out of his doom. Man will be saved when he hears the call and responds to God. God speaks to him. In the Scripture there are two phases of speaking to man. In the first place, God revealed His will in the law. And the history of Israel simply shows that man, even when delivered and kept by the grace of God, did not obey. This is where the law of Moses failed — showing man what to do was not good enough. Then there was a second revelation in the Bible, and this is the one our attention is brought to now. This is the revelation of God's further plan and we have the grace of Christ which shows how it will be done. Christ Jesus offered to save and live in anyone who believed in Him. The record of the work of Christ through the Holy Spirit in the New Testament shows how believers with the Holy Spirit operative in them can do the will of God.

> For this is the covenant that I will make with the house of Israel after those days, saith the Lord; I will put my laws into their mind, and write them in their hearts: and I will be to them a God, and they shall be to me a people (Heb. 8:10).

How will He put His laws into their minds and write them in their hearts? By giving them the Holy Spirit of Jesus Christ. Christ, the hope of glory, will dwell in them, and they will be moved to do the will of God. The reason they will not have to teach every man is because they will know. Christ Jesus will be in them. "I will be merciful to their unrighteousness, and their sins and their iniquities will I remember no more." This is the promise — the wonderful salvation believers have in Christ Jesus.

Chapter 24

BEYOND FORGIVENESS

Do you realize there is something more in spiritual blessing than to be forgiven?

> The Holy Ghost this signifying, that the way into the holiest of all was not yet made manifest, while as the first tabernacle was yet standing (Heb. 9:8).

In this epistle we have the continuing emphasis that in Christ Jesus the believer has more blessing available than could have been received under the law of Moses. The New Testament following the Old Testament does not invalidate the Old Testament. It leads the believer to more than he ever had before, and this truth has been set forth in the book of Hebrews over and over again. In this portion attention is focused upon the tabernacle, the place where the Hebrews came to worship God.

When the tribes of Israel camped in the wilderness, they settled down in such a way that they formed a square — three tribes to the north, three tribes to the east, three tribes to the south and three tribes to the west. In the middle of the camp was the tabernacle, the place of worship, which was built according to a pattern shown to Moses on Mt. Sinai. This structure was very significant, symbolizing conditions involved when a sinner comes to God. You will recall that the tabernacle was a sort of rectangular tent covered with badger skins. The inside was brilliant in color, with dyed cloth of various kinds. The tabernacle was divided into two parts. The first part where the priest entered was a room called the Holy Place or sanctuary. Two side walls upheld the roof, and one end was open while the other end was a veil or curtain through which one entered the second room called the Holiest of Holies.

When the priest came to lead the worship, he followed two procedures — the normal procedure that occurred every day and an unusual procedure that happened once a year.

The tabernacle was described in the first five verses of Chapter 9.

> Then verily the first covenant had also ordinances (ways of doing things) of divine service, (divine worship) and a worldly sanctuary (Heb. 9:1).

That word "worldly" could be misleading. It means the sanctuary was built in this world of skin and cloth like a tent, and afterwards it was built in a temple of stones and wood. You and I know that God dwelleth not in temples made with hands because He is actually living in heaven. So this worldly sanctuary is an earthly building and is simply a representation of the eternal heavenly reality.

> For there was a tabernacle made; the first, wherein was the candlestick, and the table, and the showbread; which is called the sanctuary. And after the second veil, the tabernacle which is called the Holiest of all; which had the golden censer, and the ark of the covenant overlaid round about with gold, wherein was the golden pot that had manna, and Aaron's rod that budded, and the tables of the covenant; and over it the cherubims of glory shadowing the mercy seat; of which we cannot now speak particularly (Heb. 9:2-5).

In the last words the writer is simply saying there is more truth which he is not interpreting at present. The worshiper could come any day and enter the first room. He would come to the altar to confess his sins. There the sacrifice would be killed, the blood would be shed, and his sin would be forgiven because the lamb would die for him. He then would come to the laver where he would be washed. Thus he would be cleansed. Then he would come by the candlestick where he had light illumination. On the other side of the room was the shewbread, which reminded him of the source of his strength. Then he would move on to the altar of incense where he would give thanks. That was as far as he would go. I suspect that is the pattern for many sincere people today.

The writer of this epistle makes it clear Aaron could bring the worshiper this far. The Old Testament could take anyone this far, as could also John the Baptist. A person could confess his sins at the altar; he would then be cleansed through the water of the Word and illuminated by the candlestick from the light of truth. He would be strengthened with the bread from heaven, as with the truth that is in the Lord Jesus Christ, and he would give thanks to God for blessing.

The unusual procedure once a year was that the high priest would go through that second veil into the very presence of God, and there he would make the atonement with God. Then he would come out and pronounce to the people that they were delivered from sin. Doubtless many people missed this atonement which occurred only once a year.

> But into the second went the high priest alone once every year, not without blood, which he offered for himself, and for the errors of the people: the Holy Ghost this signifying, that the way into the holiest of all was not yet made manifest, while as the first tabernacle was yet standing (Heb. 9:7-8).

What the writer emphasizes is that because of the ministry of the Levitical priesthood they knew about coming through the first room, but in Christ Jesus they could come into the very presence of God.

Chapter 25

BY THE RESURRECTION CHRIST PROVIDES GRACE TO LIVE IN NEWNESS OF LIFE

Have you understood that when Jesus Christ died for sinners He did more than suffer the penalties for sin?

We are noticing how Christ has done and continues to do more for us as our High Priest unto God, than Aaron could do when he was serving in the tabernacle here on earth. The book of Hebrews is dealing with the whole problem of our relationship to Almighty God in the Lord Jesus Christ. Apparently these believers to whom the book of Hebrews was written were people who were acquainted with the requirements and promises of the law and everything that had been taught in the temple by those who had the Old Testament law. The writer was anxious that as believers they should keep in mind there was more available for them in Christ Jesus.

There is a continuation of this emphasis throughout this book.

> Which was a figure for the time then present, in which were offered both gifts and sacrifices, that could not make him that did the service perfect, as pertaining to the conscience; which stood only in meats and drinks, and divers washings, and carnal ordinances, imposed on them until the time of reformation (Heb. 9:9-10).

Here is recognized that there was a limitation to the effectiveness of those sacrifices of animals. A man would confess his sin on the head of the animal being offered as a sacrifice, and thus be accepted of God, but that would not affect his conscience. This could also be translated "consciousness," "in his awareness" as it were, because the offering for sin would not affect his inward disposition which would be the same as before.

> But Christ being come a high priest of good things to come, by a greater and more perfect tabernacle, not made with hands, that is to say, not of this building; neither by the blood of goats and calves, but by his own blood he entered in once into the holy place, having obtained eternal redemption for us (Heb. 9:11-12).

The writer now points out that the blood of Christ Jesus was different. The blood of animals would cleanse the flesh from the guilt of the past, but nothing was done about what the man would do in the future.

> For if the blood of bulls and of goats, and the ashes of a heifer sprinkling the unclean, sanctifieth to the purifying of the flesh: how much more shall the blood of Christ, who through the eternal Spirit offered himself without spot to God, purge your conscience from dead works to serve the living God? (Heb. 9:13-14).

It is the blood of Christ that purges the conscience and changes the inward awareness and intentions from dead works to serve the living and true God. This is referring to the fact that a change will occur in the worshiper when he comes by the way of the Lord Jesus Christ. The chief difference here is that the Lord Jesus Christ having died, rose again from the dead; therefore, when He offers Himself, He is offering for the future. He offered Himself to die and be raised from the dead that He might serve in saving all who come to Him.

The person who believes in the Lord Jesus Christ offers the blood of Christ's body for past sins. Because the body of Christ is raised from the dead to live in the future the believer who is united with Him by faith has the prospect of doing the will of God. In speaking of this we cannot omit the truth of the resurrection. It was the resurrection of the Lord Jesus Christ that made His sacrifice the better one. The Lord Jesus Christ died for the sins of the past and rose again from the dead to live in the newness of life. Any person believing in Him will be raised from the dead to live unto God also.

Chapter 26

THE POWER TO PRODUCE THE NEWNESS OF LIFE MAKES THE DEATH OF CHRIST THE BETTER SACRIFICE

Is it clear to you why the death of Jesus of Nazareth was the better sacrifice?

It is hard for some to understand how studying about the blood of animals has anything to do with our daily lives. Through the sacrifice of animals God was teaching the Old Testament people that sin could be forgiven if there was death of a substitute. This death would be a sacrifice offered in place of the sinner. The Bible deals with the problem of reconciling a sinful man to the holy God. The Bible does not make man a sinner — man is naturally a sinner. The Bible does not make God holy — God *is* holy. There is a gulf between man and God, because man is sinful and God is holy. The Bible reveals how the two can be reconciled. Men, created in the image of God, sinned and came short of the glory of God, but God so loved the world that He gave His only begotten Son, offering Him as a sacrifice so that sinners by believing in Him could be saved.

The blood of the sacrifice is the clue to the reconciliation whereby the sinner can come into the presence of God. This is told over and over in the Bible. The whole worship ritual of the Levites that was conducted first in the tabernacle and afterwards in the temple showed this pattern, and this is the pattern Christ Jesus followed when He came. The New Testament tells us that in the fullness of time God sent forth His Son. God sent Him forth to die that He should be a sacrifice on our behalf. When Christ died for sinners, He did more for them than the animal sacrifices could do for the Old Testament people.

The Lord Jesus Christ in His death does more about guilt than the blood of the animals did in the Old Testament. When Christ Jesus died for the sinner and he received that death on his behalf, his sin is forgiven and his guilt is removed. This is precisely what was done about guilt in the Old Testament.

But in this New Testament procedure when Christ Jesus died for the sinner, the believer can now be delivered by this death and resurrection into a new and different life.

> And for this cause he is the mediator of the new testament, that by means of death, for the redemption of the transgressions that were under the first testament, they which are called might receive the promise of eternal inheritance (Heb. 9:15).

Christ Jesus is "the mediator" and "death" here refers to His own death on Calvary. The death of the Son of God was tragically necessary and real:

> For where a testament is, there must also of necessity be the death of the testator. For a testament is of force after men are dead: otherwise it is of no strength at all while the testator liveth . . . And almost all things are by the law purged with blood; and without shedding of blood is no remission (Heb. 9:16-22).

This is the message of the gospel. Christ Jesus died, and the sins of believers are remitted.

> It was therefore necessary that the patterns of things in the heavens should be purified with these; but the heavenly things themselves with better sacrifices than these (Heb. 9:23).

The first part of this verse speaks of the Old Testament patterns, the animal sacrifices which were offered in the tabernacle. But the heavenly things themselves in the very presence of God were based upon better sacrifices than these. Christ Jesus was the better sacrifice:

> For Christ is not entered into the holy places made with hands, which are the figures of the true; but into heaven itself, now to appear in the presence of God for us (Heb. 9:24).

Christ Jesus did not come to offer Himself in the worship in the tabernacle which presented the figures of the truth and the examples of the real thing, but He entered into heaven itself.

> Nor yet that he should offer himself often, as the high priest entereth into the holy place every year with blood of others; for then must he often have suffered since the foundation of the world: but now once in the end of the world hath he appeared to put away sin by the sacrifice of himself (Heb. 9:25-26).

He does not have to repeat this sacrifice over and over. Once for all Christ takes away the guilt and puts away the sin.

And as it is appointed unto men once to die, but after this the judgment: so Christ was once offered to bear the sins of many; and unto them that look for him shall he appear the second time without sin unto salvation (Heb. 9:27-28).

This may all seem strange in contemporary culture, yet all the way through the great impression is clear that in Christ Jesus there is something new for the believer. It will be the life of God in him.

Chapter 27

BEING WILLING TO OBEY
IS BETTER THAN DOING WHAT I CAN

Do you realize you have more to give to the Lord than that which you hold in your hand?

"Then said I, Lo, I come to do thy will, O God."

The history of spiritual experience shows how a person generally is inclined to think that he should do right in God's sight. That seems so simple. I suspect a good many of us, when we think in terms of doing what God wants us to do, may think He wants us to go to church. And He does. We will join in singing the hymns, and He wants us to share at the time of prayer. When the Word of God is read and discussed we will listen and receive it as such. Do you realize that the matter of going to church for that hour is not enough; that is simply an outward token of what should be inwardly done. Can I keep in mind that whereas I worship God in church (and this is perfectly right) I should also worship God every moment and every hour of every day? I should always walk in the presence of God, and I should bow down my heart to Him in prayer at times throughout the day. Moment by moment as I live I should be conscious of His will at all times.

The book of Hebrews emphasizes that the outward responses — our actions in worship services — are tokens, gestures of what we should have in our hearts. The wedding ceremony, in which certain questions are asked of the bride and the groom, does not mean all is done once and for all. There is a sense in which it has been done once and for all, but when the minister asks this man if he will have this woman to be his lawful wedded wife, he means not only in this ten or fifteen minute ceremony, but will this be true forever and ever? What God wants is a continuing response to Him. It is natural to ask: "What wilt thou have me to do?" Then we can expect to receive certain instructions; but there is more than that. If we were to construct a building we would need plans and specifications, but we would also need a foreman to see that the plans are followed. This is what the book of Hebrews indicates. Spiritually speaking, the plans and regulations are set out in the law of the Old Testament, but the gospel brings in the Master Builder, the One who will lead in these ways of the law.

This study in the epistle to the Hebrews now focuses attention upon the form of the offering. Again it is pointed out there is a better offering in Christ Jesus than there was in the Old Testament procedure. The limitation, the inadequacy, in the Old Testament procedure is pointed out.

> For the law having a shadow of good things to come, and not the very image of the things, can never with those sacrifices which they offered year by year continually make the comers thereunto perfect (Heb. 10:1).

"The law" is the Old Testament revelation. "Having a shadow of good things to come" indicates the Old Testament law was promising the blessing of God. However, the law could not show the whole truth because, Christ had not yet come. The writer presents his argument:

> For then would they not have ceased to be offered? (If they had made them perfect and complete they would not have had to offer again) because that the worshipers once purged should have had no more conscience of sins. But in those sacrifices there is a remembrance again made of sins every year (Heb. 10:2-3).

Why was the procedure being followed every year? Because while it was never complete it was yet showing how one day it would be done. The writer concedes:

> For it is not possible that the blood of bulls and of goats should take away sins (Heb. 10:4).

This sacrificing of the blood of lambs and goats would take away guilt, but it could not take away sin — the inward disposition to do wrong. The better procedure was revealed by Jesus Christ.

> Wherefore when he cometh into the world, he saith, Sacrifice and offering thou wouldest not, but a body hast thou prepared me: in burnt offerings and sacrifices for sin thou hast had no pleasure. Then said I, Lo, I come (in the volume of the book it is written of me) to do thy will, O God (Heb. 10:5-7).

These verses speak of the Lord Jesus Christ when it is pointed out that sacrifice and offering as specified in the Old Testament were merely tokens of what needed to be done. In themselves this was actually not what God wanted. The Lord Jesus Christ says He will bring His body to obey, not something in His hands. As the lamb was brought for a token, so the Lord Jesus would come and yield Himself — this is the crux of this epistle.

Chapter 28

AS A MAN THINKETH IN HIS HEART, SO IS HE

Can you understand that the disposition to want to be well-pleasing to God is more important than doing what I am told to do?

This particular study will require considerable attention inasmuch as it is not a simple line of thought. However it is very important; it shows that Christ Jesus, when we believe in Him, does more for us than rules and regulations can possibly do. The real truth is that I am in myself a sinner and God is holy; God makes it possible for me to come. He does this through the Lord Jesus Christ whom He sends to be my Savior and my Lord. Christ comes as my sacrifice and He is also the one in whom I am to live.

What we have in record about Jesus of Nazareth is that of a child of God obeying Him. This is the picture. Being in the form of man He did not so much demonstrate a sinner who will die because of sin, as He did a child of God who will live and obey God. It is here the idea of a substitute for the sinner is brought in. A substitute is offered who obeys for the believer. The record shows Christ Jesus obeying God in living and dying. Inasmuch as Christ did this for the believer, the believer should obey God. Christ Jesus obeyed God for him; now Christ obeys the Father in him. That is the way it works.

> Above when he said, Sacrifice and offering and burnt offerings and offering for sin thou wouldest not, neither hadst pleasure therein; which are offered by the law; then said he, Lo, I come to do thy will, O God. He taketh away the first, that he may establish the second. By the which will we are sanctified through the offering of the body of Jesus Christ once for all (Heb. 10:8-10).

"By the which will" — God's will, which Jesus Christ came to do. Believers are sanctified through the offering of the body of Jesus Christ once for all, to serve God by the will of the Lord Jesus Christ. "I come to do thy will" — doing the will of God on the part of the Lord Jesus Christ causes believers to be sanctified. This comes through the offering of the body of the Lord Jesus Christ once for all. Now the offering of the body was done by the Lord Jesus Christ on Calvary's cross. The Lord Jesus offered His body again when it was buried in the grave, and again in the resurrection, and again in the ascension into heaven. He is now in that body in the presence of God, exercising His will to do the will of God.

How does this operate? By the Holy Spirit, Christ shares with the believer His will to do the will of God, and it is in His own obedience that the will of Christ is actually activated in believers now by the indwelling Holy Spirit of God.

> And every priest standeth daily ministering and offering oftentimes the same sacrifices, which can never take away sins: but this man, after he had offered one sacrifice for sins for ever, sat down on the right hand of God; from henceforth expecting till his enemies be made his footstool. For by one offering he hath perfected for ever them that are sanctified. Whereof the Holy Ghost also is a witness to us: for after that he had said before, This is the covenant that I will make with them after those days, saith the Lord; I will put my laws into their hearts, and in their minds will I write them; and their sins and iniquities will I remember no more. Now where remission of these is, there is no more offering for sin (Heb. 10:11-18).

These words confirm the fact that with the Lord Jesus Christ in the presence of God right now this is the situation: His body was yielded to God and given for sin; He took the believer's place. His body is now willing to do the will of God, and the believer is involved in that. That disposition to want to do the will of God is brought into the believer by the indwelling of the Holy Spirit. In other words, having completely obeyed His Father in His own body as Jesus of Nazareth (He learned obedience by the things He suffered) He now shares this committed attitude of obedience which He learned at Gethsemane with believers, who are now in Him by the grace of God and are made mature in Him forever. This is the spiritual operation of God's work of salvation in the believer.

The important fact is: Christ Jesus is in the believer. He is actually doing the will of the Father through the believer.

Chapter 29

DOING IS BETTER THAN KNOWING WHAT TO DO

Do you realize that the gospel of salvation offers to believers far more than instruction as to what to do?

Let us hold fast the profession of our faith without wavering (Heb. 10:23).

Believers make a good start when they confess their sins; that is the first step one must take. But believers can do still better than that when they yield to the living Lord Jesus Christ. This, of course, includes the confessing of their sins, but far more, it includes the receiving of Jesus Christ into their hearts. Thus we would say on the one hand that when the believer views Christ as Savior that is good, but when he views Christ as Lord, that is better. In a very simple way it can be expressed something like this: Subscribing to a worthwhile cause is good — making payment is better.

There are two centers of concern in our relationship with the Lord. One is our sin, and the other is the obedience He wants us to give to Him. We know that so far as our sins are concerned, they lead unto death: "The wages of sin is death." On the other hand our obedience leads unto life: "For whosoever doeth the will of God abideth forever." Both statements are valid, but how different they are! When you think in terms of obedience you know that life is ahead of you. In order to provide for the confessing of sins and the yielding to Christ, this general truth is set forth in Scripture: God will provide Himself a sacrifice. He will provide Himself a substitute who will function in a way that will enable the Lord to bring His will to pass. When we want to deal with sin on the one hand and obedience on the other, we must have something moving toward death and something moving toward life. In order to take care of all this, God will provide Himself a sacrifice; in this case He has provided one who will fill both. God has prepared Christ a body in which He could

87

serve God, so Christ comes to His Father saying: "Lo, I come to do thy will, O God." In willing obedience He comes to obey God, and now there is the living sacrifice. He not only is a sacrifice in the sense that He died for sin, but He is raised from the dead and continues on as a sacrifice, giving Himself over in willing obedience to His Father.

In this is found everything that is included at Pentecost when the Spirit of God came into the human form of the disciples. Earlier than this the Spirit of God had come into the human form of Jesus of Nazareth and had moved Him to perfect obedience, which marked His life here upon earth. So we have in the first place, with reference to sin, everything that is pictured leading up to Calvary, and in the second place with reference to life, everything that leads to Pentecost.

In reference to the whole picture is this statement in Scripture: "To obey is better than sacrifice." In Christ Jesus, God has arranged that so far as sin is concerned, by way of Calvary believers can be forgiven; and insofar as life is concerned, by the way of Pentecost believers will find themselves inwardly moved to be obedient. Thus they are able to understand what is involved in this way: It is not what I bring in my hand as a gift or sacrifice to God, but it is my hand yielded to God that is satisfying to Him. This brings out the truth of that Old Testament Scripture: "To obey is better than sacrifice."

> Having therefore, brethren, boldness to enter into the holiest by the blood of Jesus, by a new and living way, which he hath consecrated for us, through the veil, that is to say, his flesh; and having a high priest over the house of God; let us draw near with a true heart in full assurance of faith, having our hearts sprinkled from an evil conscience, and our bodies washed with pure water (Heb. 10:19-22).

Believers can come into the presence of God in the fullest confidence.

> Let us hold fast the profession of our faith without wavering; (for he is faithful that promised;) and let us consider one another to provoke unto love and to good works: not forsaking the assembling of ourselves together, as the manner of some is; but exhorting one another: and so much the more, as ye see the day approaching (Heb. 10:23-25).

In Christ Jesus believers are able to move forward in His will and to do the will of God.

Chapter 30

DISOBEDIENCE IS DANGEROUS

Do you realize that knowing what to do makes a man responsible to do what ought to be done?

> For if we sin willfully after that we have received the knowledge of
> the truth, there remaineth no more sacrifice for sins (Heb. 10:26).

The discussion of spiritual living in this epistle has been featured by emphasis upon the wonderful grace of God in Christ. But now and again the writer raises a warning note. It is true that God in grace provides all that is needed for blessing, but no one should allow himself to think that God is not sensitive to disobedience.

In mercy God may be very gracious toward weakness and inability, but it is never true that He will tolerate carelessness or willful disobedience. In his epistle to the Galatians Paul likens the believer living in the new covenant to a son who has graduated from being led by a tutor or a governor and has now entered into the privileges of being a son and heir in the family. In this epistle to the Hebrews the writer is warning the believer who is living in the blessing of the new covenant that obedience to God is just as surely expected and required in the new covenant as it ever was in the old covenant. Jesus of Nazareth said, "I do all things to please my Father." When the Holy Spirit is operative in the believer in the new covenant, He activates the will of Christ the Lord in the heart. "Christ in you" will mean careful, sincere obedience to the will of God.

> But a certain fearful looking for of judgment and fiery indignation,
> which shall devour the adversaries (Heb. 10:27).

The New Covenant is altogether of grace. But this does not imply that the law of God has been discontinued or is changed. "God is not mocked." He will judge and destroy whatever or whoever is contrary to His will. It is proper that any human being should quail before the wrath of God.

"God is angry with the wicked every day." It is true that "all have sinned and come short of the glory of God." And "the soul that sinneth it shall die." But in mercy God has promised salvation for sinners through Christ. And now God "commandeth all men everywhere to repent." It is true that "whosoever will may come" and that God is no respecter of persons, but it is also true that "God resisteth the proud."

The writer of this epistle has been emphasizing the marvelous grace of God in which salvation to the uttermost is provided for all who believe. But at this point in the epistle he chooses to warn earnestly that no reader shall fall into the snare of thinking that God is soft in His attitude toward disobedience. The testimony in Scripture is clear.

> He that despised Moses' law died without mercy under two or three witnesses (Heb. 10:28).

God is forever the same. Any suggestion that His attitude toward sin is different in New Testament times from what it was in Old Testament times is definitely an error.

The very fact that God has revealed Himself so graciously in the incarnation and the ministry of the Son of God makes the sin of disobedience even more heinous. The soul that has heard the gospel and turns away in disobedience has no basis for thinking there will be any escape from judgment at the hands of God.

> Of how much sorer punishment, suppose ye, shall he be thought worthy, who hath trodden under foot the Son of God, and hath counted the blood of the covenant, wherewith he was sanctified, an unholy thing, and hath done despite unto the Spirit of grace? (Heb. 10:29).

These words may disturb some readers who may be perplexed about the possibility of one who has been sanctified by the blood of the covenant turning away from God. But real caution should be exercised lest we fall into the snare of rendering a statement of the Lord meaningless by our interpretation of Scripture as a whole. No doubt the believer in Christ as a born again child of God has wonderful blessings and rich privileges, but there will never be a situation in which anyone by clever interpretation of Scripture can hold that God will be obligated to bless an unfaithful person.

The sound meaning of any Scripture can be recognized by comparing Scripture with Scripture. Our minds are so partial and words are so limited that misunderstanding is always a liability. Even in this instance the writer leads the reader to call to mind other Scriptures that will make his meaning clear.

> For we know him that hath said, Vengeance belongeth unto me, I
> will recompense, saith the Lord. And again, The Lord shall judge
> his people (Heb. 10:30).

Whatever may be true about God's attitude toward all men who are His
creatures and whom He judges every day, this is not the point in this
portion of the revelation. The writer is directing his warning to persons
who have heard the gospel and "have tasted the good Word of God, and
the powers of the world to come." He is not accusing any such of having
turned away, but he is warning them of the dire consequences that
threaten any such apostasy.

> It is a fearful thing to fall into the hands of the living God (Heb.
> 10:31).

Several times during this epistle the writer has challenged his readers with
such warning (Heb. 2:2-4; 6:4-6; 10:28-31). At no time does he say that
true believers have turned away, but the thrust of his direct emphasis is so
plain that no one should let such warning fall to the ground as mere idle
words.

Chapter 31

THE IMPORTANCE OF BEING PERSISTENT

What would you say that a person should do after he has done what is right and good?

> For ye have need of patience, that, after ye have done the will of God, ye might receive the promise (Heb. 10:36).

My answer to the above question would be: Hang on! Do not let up now. If you have done that which is right and good, stay in there. Thus far we have been dealing with matters of interpretation, learning how we should view Jesus Christ, and how we should appreciate the work He has done and which is being done now by the Levitical priesthood as they seek to carry out the Old Testament instructions.

How shall you understand what it is to live according to regulations, and how shall you appreciate what it is to live in personal fellowship and communion with the Lord Jesus Christ? There have been doctrines set forth and discussions of these doctrines as to the ways of God's operation in salvation and finally, coming to the climax, we have learned how the human being turns to God and receives the Lord Jesus to work in him what is well pleasing in His sight. To have the living Lord working in the believer according to the Holy Spirit, by the Holy Spirit, is the goal toward which God's plan moves. This is what has been set forth over and over.

Now we shall turn to a practical aspect of this whole matter. We shall take a look at the actual achievement of these matters. We shall look at the more practical aspect by asking what shall the believer do in response to this truth about the will of God. We have in mind that some believe in the Lord and want His will to be done. Now we shall see that what they are to do is to endure, to continue in their believing despite opposition.

> But call to remembrance the former days, in which, after ye were illuminated, ye endured a great fight of afflictions; partly, whilst ye

were made a gazingstock both by reproaches and afflictions; and
partly, whilst ye became companions of them that were so used. For
ye had compassion of me in my bonds. (Heb. 10:32-34a).

Apparently the writer to the Hebrews had been among them and he had
been arrested and treated contemptuously by the society in which they
were living, and they had had compassion upon him. They shared with
him in the shameful treatment to which he had been subjected.

"And took joyfully the spoiling of your goods." This word "spoiling" could best be understood if it had been translated "despoiling." By
spoiling it means to say that others came and took the goods of these
believers off like booty in a battle, so referring to this loss as being as the
fortunes of war. These people had not fought against this loss: "Knowing
in yourselves that ye have in heaven a better and an enduring substance."
It is worthwhile to notice here that the Lord God did not interfere with the
treatment they received. Despite the fact that their property was being
taken away from them and their holdings despoiled, God allowed these
things to happen, yet they had compassion on this minister, the writer:
"For ye had compassion of me in my bonds" (Heb. 10:34).

This is a description of the wonderful attitude that believers have when
they suffer loss because of their testimony.

> Cast not away therefore your confidence, which hath great recom-
> pense of reward (Heb. 10:35).

There is always the danger that after the believer has done well he will
become discouraged and will quit; the writer did not want them to do this.
After they had done what they should have done, and were confident
when they did it, he wanted them to keep that confidence up.

> For ye have need of patience, that, after ye have done the will of
> God, ye might receive the promise (Heb. 10:36).

The writer reminded them that they have need of the kind of patience that
will lead them on in the way they were going, without hesitation. They
needed to persevere in order that they might receive the promise.

Between the time a believer does what he should do and the time he
gets what he felt was coming to him there may be a time element. There
was a time element with them. A believer has need of patience that after
he has done the will of God, he might receive the promise. Whatever the
will of God was for them in the way in which they identified themselves
with the name of the Lord Jesus Christ, whatever they had done publicly
in any way to draw attention to themselves in any critical fashion, they
could now have in mind that if they would keep on steadfastly in the

position they took, the promise would surely come to them. God would surely bless them.

> For yet a little while, and he that shall come will come, and will not tarry (Heb. 10:37).

Some people use this verse to indicate something with regard to the coming of the Lord at the end of the world, in the fashion of eschatology. I will not use it that way. I think this verse means simply that if a believer puts his trust in the Lord and serves Him, God will bless him. The verse does not promise He will bless the believer today, but it does assure him that God will bless him. He will need to have patience and wait a little while, but God will actually bless him.

In this portion there is a great verse that was first found in the Old Testament, and which has been especially meaningful to Protestants. Many call it Martin Luther's verse because it meant so much to him: "The just shall live by faith" (Heb. 10:38). The emphasis upon "the just" is the reason it meant so much to Luther, who believed it is vital to be right in God's sight. That person shall live by faith and not by works. There have been others, also, who have been impressed by this verse. I have always felt that John Wesley would emphasize the word "live." I am not sure we have an outstanding leader in our time who lays emphasis on "faith." But all three emphases are true. The person who is right, who is just and acceptable unto God, shall live so far as his actual experience is concerned, by faith, by trusting in God.

Faith is persistent. The believer stays right in there until God comes through with His promises. If any man draws back, if he believes for awhile and then quits, "my soul shall have no pleasure in him."

> But we are not of them who draw back unto perdition; but of them that believe to the saving of the soul (Heb. 10:39).

You and I have need of patience in order that we may continue in our obedience and in our trust, that we may be blessed.

Chapter 32

THE NATURE OF FAITH

Do you know what faith really is?

> But without faith it is impossible to please him: for he that cometh to God must believe that he is, and that he is a rewarder of them that diligently seek him (Heb. 11:6).

It is a common saying that salvation is by faith. No doubt it is just as widely known that the gospel of the Lord Jesus Christ calls upon men to believe in God. The writer of this epistle has been presenting the idea that greater benefits are available to people who live in the Lord Jesus Christ by faith in Him, than there are for those who try only to keep rules and regulations of right conduct. Of course, doing what is right is in itself a good thing, and the rules and regulations of right conduct, of righteousness are holy and just and good. But human nature being what it is, men find themselves weak and unable to do the right things even when they know what to do, so we are brought face to face with a marvelous provision in the gospel of Jesus Christ: God sent His Son into the world to do perfectly what the will of God is, and to provide for believers in Christ Jesus a substitute life that they can have from Him. Most of this epistle has been doctrinal. There has been discussion of the truth that there is something better available for believers in Christ Jesus than they would have if they just did what they thought was right.

The writer now moves on to think about practical matters because all the discussion has led to the conclusion that by faith in Christ Jesus a believer can actually receive from Him that which will bring him into the full measure of God's will, that he might be fully blessed of God. There is here a classic statement about faith:

> Now faith is the substance of things hoped for, the evidence of things not seen (Heb. 11:1).

In this statement can be seen aspects of faith: things hoped for, and things not seen. "Things hoped for" refers to things that are not here as yet, and "things which are not seen" refers to things which are not in sight. Notice in each case there are actually *things*. These may be distant and may not yet be, but they are actual and real. Faith is the actual realization (taking them as real), the evidence of the reality of things that are not yet (they are hoped for) and things that are not seen (they are distant but real).

When I try to understand faith for myself I always think of radar as an illustration. This electronic device enables the pilot of an airplane to get in touch with things that are so distant he cannot see them. These things are out of sight, yet they are really there. Radar does not imagine things. It actually bounces off objects that are really out there in the world although they are out of sight. So faith lays hold on things that are real even though they are not now to be seen and in some cases have not yet happened. The reason they are real is because they are in the will of God. In this connection the oldtimers in Scripture, the men who are the fathers of Israel, actually had a good report. The source of their achievements was their belief in God. The writer then makes a statement that I fear is generally ignored:

> Through faith we understand that the worlds were framed by the word of God, so that things which are seen were not made of things which do appear (Heb. 11:3).

Here it is indicated that the creation of the world did not take place by natural processes of elements that are now in the world. The actual form and structure of the world was by the Word of God. If you should look at a big church building you would see that it has a certain design — the walls are built in a certain way, and the roof in a certain way; the towers are placed in a certain way and the windows are set in a certain fashion. Can you understand that the design did not come out of the stone; the architect is the one who is credited with the design. So it is when we look at the world. We will not understand the nature of the world by examining its elements or by analyzing it according to its physical and chemical structures. We understand by faith, by what is revealed to us in the Scriptures — the world was framed by the Word of God. So the things we see are not made of things which do appear; they did not originate out of natural processes.

> By faith Abel offered unto God a more excellent sacrifice than Cain, by which he obtained witness that he was righteous, God testifying of his gifts: and by it he being dead yet speaketh (Heb. 11:4).

Abel must have understood something that God wanted him to do and acted accordingly. If Cain understood it, he did not act that way. The difference between Cain and Abel was that their works were different. The works of Abel were such that God did approve and the works of Cain were such that God did not approve. It seems probable that what made the difference was that one acted in obedience and the other did not.

> By faith Enoch was translated that he should not see death; and was not found, because God had translated him: for before his translation he had this testimony, that he pleased God. But without faith it is impossible to please him: for he that cometh to God must believe that he is, and that he is a rewarder of them that diligently seek him (Heb. 11:5-6).

It is obvious that if you are going to believe that God is, you have a problem — you have not seen Him. He is invisible, yet you must take Him to be real, and that He is a rewarder of them that diligently seek Him. You have not seen Him operate yet you trust Him. This is the way in which faith works.

"By faith Noah, being warned of God of things not seen as yet . . ." (Heb. 11:7). The things were real (the flood actually came) but it had not yet occurred when God told Noah it was going to come. Because Noah believed God about something that had not yet happened, he was moved to take certain action which resulted in his salvation. By that action he condemned others because they did not respond to the Word of God.

> By faith Abraham, when he was called to go out into a place which he should after receive for an inheritance, obeyed; and he went out, not knowing whither he went (Heb. 11:8).

The basis of his confidence was not upon anything he could see, but upon the Word of God. We have been following this one idea all the way through: When we act in faith we do not go by the things that are apparent, but by what has been revealed. The Word of God is our guide and we trust in Him.

Chapter 33

THE DESCENDANTS OF ABRAHAM
BELIEVED THE PROMISES OF GOD

Do you understand that saving faith for the believer is a matter of taking for real the things which have been revealed by the Word of God?

> These all died in faith, not having received the promises, but having seen them afar off, and were persuaded of them, and embraced them, and confessed that they were strangers and pilgrims on the earth (Heb. 11:13).

These words refer to the descendants of Abraham. Our attention is being focused upon faith — believing the promises of God and taking as true what we cannot see, but what God has told us is real. God tells us what He will do and we can believe Him. He has offered Jesus Christ as our Savior and Lord, telling us Christ will bear away our sins. He has given us to understand that if we believe in Christ we will be born again, and by the grace of God be made into the children of God. All of this is offered to us through the Scriptures for our information and for our response in faith.

By way of helping us to respond intelligently we have here a discussion of the examples of the fathers of Israel who believed in God. Abraham, when he was called, went into a place he did not know about, confident because he knew the Lord.

> By faith he sojourned in the land of promise, as in a strange country, dwelling in tabernacles with Isaac and Jacob, the heirs with him of the same promise: for he looked for a city which hath foundations, whose builder and maker is God (Heb. 11:9-10).

"Sojourned" means he dwelt there temporarily. He lived there like a tourist, passing through. The structures were temporary. Living in this world Abraham was not influenced by what he saw. He lived in his heart and spirit by what God told him. He treated this world like a temporary place — something he was passing through — and while he was in this world he never built a permanent place of residence. He used only tents because "he looked for a city which hath foundations." He looked for a dwelling place which was really solid and sure, "whose builder and maker is God." The men of Babel undertook to build a tower and a city lest they be scattered. They intended to make a permanent dwelling place. God frustrated them and foiled them in their purpose. They never did finish it. The very next chapter tells about Abraham, who was different from the men of Babel. He lived in temporary structures and always treated this world like a strange place, because he was looking for something else.

> Through faith also Sarah herself received strength to conceive seed, and was delivered of a child when she was past age, because she judged him faithful who had promised (Heb. 11:11).

Chapter 4 in Romans tells about Abraham:

> And being not weak in faith, he considered not his own body now dead, when he was about a hundred years old, neither yet the deadness of Sarah's womb: he staggered not at the promise of God through unbelief; but was strong in faith, giving glory to God; and being fully persuaded that, what he had promised, he was able also to perform (Rom. 4:19-21).

Sarah and Abraham believed God and Isaac was born.

> Therefore sprang there even of one, and him as good as dead, so many as the stars of the sky in multitude, and as the sand which is by the seashore innumerable (Heb. 11:12).

This refers to the descendants of Abraham through Isaac who were born because Isaac was born, and Isaac was born because of the faith of Abraham and Sarah.

> These all died in faith, not having received the promises, but having seen them afar off, and were persuaded of them, and embraced them, and confessed that they were strangers and pilgrims on the earth (Heb. 11:13).

These people lived and died believing in the invisible God and His promises. They never did actually receive the full measure of what God promised them. The record tells of the character, the frame of mind, the whole attitude of these people of faith. They treated this world like a secondary place. This is the way it should be with all believers. The believer's "citizenship is in heaven" and he counts himself in this world as a stranger and a pilgrim on the earth. Peter uses this language when he urges:

> Dearly beloved, I beseech you as strangers and pilgrims, abstain from fleshly lusts, which war against the soul (1 Pet. 2:11).

It has always been the character of believing people to look at this world as something temporary. They place their hope and confidence in God.

> For they that say such things declare plainly that they seek a country. And truly, if they had been mindful of that country from whence they came out, they might have had opportunity to have returned (Heb. 11:14-15).

The descendants of Abraham were not satisfied with the land they were passing through. Their action in going forward was voluntary; they could have returned to the land of their origin if they had wanted to do that. Just so a believer can go back into the world if he wants to; the world would be glad to have him back. But if he has faith in God he will seek the things of God apart from the things of the world.

> But now they desire a better country, that is, an heavenly: wherefore God is not ashamed to be called their God: for he hath prepared for them a city (Heb. 11:16).

This is the way God feels about people living in this world. They should consider this world to be secondary.

> By faith Abraham, when he was tried, offered up Isaac: and he that had received the promises offered up his only begotten son, of whom it was said, That in Isaac shall thy seed be called (Heb. 11:17-18).

The point made here was that although Abraham was expecting many descendants from Isaac, yet he offered up Isaac. He did this because God asked him to do so. He acted in obedience to God.

> Accounting that God was able to raise him up, even from the dead; from whence also he received him in a figure (Heb. 11:19).

> By faith Isaac blessed Jacob and Esau concerning things to come (Heb. 11:20).

When Isaac blessed his two sons regarding their futures, he did not know about the future; he had not been there. Yet he told them things that would happen because he believed in God.

> By faith Jacob, when he was a-dying, blessed both the sons of Joseph; and worshiped, leaning upon the top of his staff (Heb. 11:21).

Jacob did this because he believed in God.

> By faith Joseph, when he died, made mention of the departing of the children of Israel; and gave commandment concerning his bones (Heb. 11:22).

When Joseph died in the land of Egypt he would not let them bury him. He instructed them to keep his bones in his coffin and take them with them when they went out of the land of Egypt into the land of Canaan. He was that sure God's Word would actually be fulfilled.

Chapter 34

BELIEVERS IN GOD ARE ALWAYS RICHLY BLESSED

Do you realize that faith is helpful only when you believe in the right thing?

> And these all, having obtained a good report through faith, received not the promise (Heb. 11:39).

These words come near the end of this long chapter in which there are glorious reports of that which was done in response to faith. Chapter 11 in Hebrews has been called by many "The Hall of Fame of Believers." Paul had written to the Ephesians that "by grace are ye saved through faith." We understand so clearly that faith is an element, the basic element in all spiritual experience. It must precede receiving any blessing at all. Each of these persons in faith did certain things because he believed in the promises of God: Noah made the ark and was spared; Abraham's faith in God moved him to obey in going out into a new country; Isaac, Jacob and Joseph were all men of faith.

Moses, through faith, received wisdom from God which enabled him to make a good choice so far as his life was concerned:

> By faith Moses, when he was come to years, refused to be called the son of Pharaoh's daughter; choosing rather to suffer affliction with the people of God, than to enjoy the pleasures of sin for a season; esteeming the reproach of Christ greater riches than the treasures in Egypt: for he had respect unto the recompense of the reward (Heb. 11:24-26).

This is the record of the great renunciation on the part of Moses. He gave himself over entirely to the promises of God. He made a choice to suffer affliction with the people of God rather than to enjoy the pleasures of sin for a season. This can be taken to show how Moses esteemed his own self, because sin will always be found in some form of serving self.

Is there anything valuable or worthwhile in selfishness? The Bible reveals what is characteristic so far as the self is concerned (1 John 2:16). We have appetites and imaginations and vanity, and along these lines we are led into that which is not useful, that which is not good for us. Our appetite is developed out of hunger. Hunger is a proper feeling, but we develop our appetites which are our own interests in any matters. Vision is a valuable faculty, but on the basis of our vision we develop imaginations which can cause many evil results. Self-consciousness seems to belong to the experience of coming of age. A person becomes aware of himself as he approaches maturity, but this can be developed into vanity. Appetite, which can be a depraved development of hunger; imagination based on vision; and vanity, which can be a depraved development of self-consciousness, constitute "the world" when taken together. This has something to offer on the one hand, but on the other hand we can look at the joys of the Lord.

What would be the joys of the Lord as we know them? To begin with, there would be communion. This communion which we have in Christ is developed out of our need for fellowship. We have this need for fellowship, and in Christ we have communion with Him and with those who belong to Him. Then there is confidence: We need help and we need encouragement; we find in the joy of the Lord our confidence in Him. This confidence which we have in Him is a real source of joy. And let us think of contentment: We have need of things, but in Christ Jesus we find ourselves content with such things as we have. Thus in thinking of the joys of the Lord, we think of communion, confidence and contentment.

By contrasting the values of self over against the joys of the Lord we can understand why our Lord Jesus asked this question: "What shall it profit a man, if he shall gain the whole world, and lose his own soul? (Mark 8:36) In gaining the whole world a man would gain money and that would arouse the cupidity of others. Other people would love what he has and they would want what he has. Covetousness would follow. Then again, if a man has the things of this world, such as money, it would give him prestige. He could easily think he is better than other people. This would arouse jealousy and that would not bring him peace. If a man should for any reason think he has power, that would generate rivals and people who would oppose him. If a man should become self-indulgent this would arouse envy. All of this would result in serving self alone.

Now let us consider the things a believer can have with Christ. He can have friends with Christ Jesus. And that is the lightest load any man will ever carry — a friend. He will never be alone. He will have helpers who will delight to help and well-wishers who will work with him. Peace with God and goodwill with men are some of the blessings in Christ. We read that Moses exercised his power of choice in the great renunciation when he set aside the things of self, choosing rather to suffer affliction with the people of God than to enjoy the pleasures of sin for a season. Such were real pleasures but he would not enjoy them ". . . esteeming the reproach of Christ greater riches than the treasures in Egypt: for he had respect unto the recompense of the reward."

Hebrews 11:32-35 records the achievement of great things by these people through faith. The last three verses are a glorious record of endurance. Some were greatly blessed with material benefits; some endured real suffering; but all received a good report through faith. Faith can operate to accomplish things and enable us to endure things pleasing unto God.

Chapter 35

TROUBLE IN THIS WORLD IS TO BE EXPECTED

Would you understand that any person living and acting in the will of God is likely to meet with trouble in personal affairs?

Let us run with patience the race that is set before us (Heb. 12:1).

The writer now outlines the guidance believers will have from God in their daily lives. Salvation comes to them in this world but it is not of this world. This salvation is the work of God, coming to believers as they live in this world, aiming to deliver them out of this world. Every person has a physical body. This body has interests in this physical world, and in these interests and these desires men are largely enmeshed. Hebrews 11 showed that some persons, because they were believers, endured much hardship. Any notion that if a person obeys the Lord everything will be easy, is just not scriptural. The Lord Jesus was perfect in doing the will of His Father, and He went to the cross of Calvary.

You and I are in this world. We feel it, and we can become attached to it, but this world is not eternal; it is temporary. If we become too involved in the things of this world, we will be hindered so far as spiritual matters are concerned. Apparently this realization is what God is working toward in His providence. The gospel presents Christ Jesus as our Savior; He is our Savior to draw us out of this world in the way one would rescue a drowning man from a lake. Now God, in His grace and in His providence, will put all things together to get us out of this world. It seems the simple strategy which the Father uses is to reveal to us the inadequacy of this world. One of the ways of showing this to us is to let us suffer. If you have a real suffering experience you will know how quickly you will feel this world is not much. You would be willing to do without that much suffering. It is as though the Lord would make a curriculum for each of us to follow, which would set before us the things we must do in order to learn the will of God. This great program we are to follow is called in this book of Hebrews: "The race that is set before us."

We may be sure we will learn about entering into blessing. We will find that we enter into this blessing as we move along in faith, trusting in God.

> Wherefore seeing we also are compassed about with so great a cloud of witnesses, let us lay aside every weight, and the sin which doth so easily beset us, and let us run with patience the race that is set before us (Heb. 12:1).

Here the writer is using the figure of a race track in some huge amphitheater. The onlookers are the witnesses referred to in chapter 11.

The language implies a runner taking off his outer garments. Believers should take off all extra things and set them aside and run with patience following the course set for them in the providence of God. This is very much like pruning the branches of a tree — unloading the nonessentials. Believers are to put away the things that do not really help them. This is not to say these nonessentials are necessarily evil. They just get in the way. Let believers lay aside considerations that are not important or helpful.

There are different opinions about " . . . the sin which doth so easily beset us." Some think this refers to sin in general because sin so easily besets us, and some think it refers to some specific sin that we have learned to call our "besetting sin." Each of us may have some special weakness. The writer is simply saying let us put all these things to one side and let us run with patience. As mentioned previously, the word *patience* means to stick on through to the end. Let us run with determination to finish, with the intention of completing the race.

> Looking unto Jesus the author and finisher of our faith; who for the joy that was set before him endured the cross, despising the shame, and is set down at the right hand of the throne of God (Heb. 12:2).

This is our example. Christ Jesus was called upon to run a certain race that led Him right to the cross of Calvary, and through the cross of Calvary right on into the very presence of His Father. The Lord Jesus, looking into the face of God, endured the cross and despised the shame of it. He is now set down at the right hand of God. That is to be our example.

> And ye have forgotten the exhortation which speaketh unto you as unto children, My son, despise not thou the chastening of the Lord, nor faint when thou art rebuked of him: for whom the Lord loveth he chasteneth, and scourgeth every son whom he receiveth (Heb. 12:5-6).

This is the way of claiming that all trouble a believer will have is under

God's control. It is quite true that the believer will have troubles. Why does trouble come and what is its meaning? There are two things that can be held in mind: The soul can be conscious of his sin, and he can think this trouble comes because of his sin and in payment thereof. Then it would be punishment. But there is another way to look at trouble. The believer is going forward in the presence of God and he will be brought into God's presence without spot and without blemish. This trouble he has can contribute to that glory. This suffering he is experiencing can actually help him in reaching the blessed purpose of God. The Lord Jesus learned obedience by suffering. The believer may learn something from the suffering he is going through. In this case, the trouble would be chastening.

Chapter 36

CHASTENING BRINGS BLESSING

Do you realize that when parents truly love their children they discipline them?

> For whom the Lord loveth he chasteneth, and scourgeth every son whom he receiveth (Heb. 12:6).

We have now an insight into the nature of the blessings of the gospel. All the way through the book of Hebrews we have noted that the writer is emphasizing there is more blessing available through the Lord Jesus Christ than there was in or by the law of Moses, and he has discussed this in various ways until at this point in the book he is discussing the actual operations involved in receiving the blessing. He has just finished a great chapter in which he has emphasized that the way to receive the blessing is by faith. In chapter 12 we learn something further: Believing in God will involve us in certain experiences in this world that are not pleasant. Actually, believing in God will involve us in things which we could count suffering and even persecution.

It is easy to understand why I would not make it my responsibility to check up on my neighbor's children. I let my neighbor's children get by with much that I would not let my own get away with. Why do I act this way? I would say because they are not mine. Every faithful parent is far more exacting with his own children than he is with the neighbor's children, because he wants his own children to improve, to be well prepared for the days ahead; so he trains them in that direction. The book of Hebrews presents this truth to help us. It is true that we live by faith in the Lord Jesus Christ and that through living in Him we draw nigh unto God. But now we shall consider that the living God arranges this so that walking in the way of the Lord Jesus Christ, living by faith in Him, will lead the believer into trouble and suffering and sorrow. We shall consider later some of the reasons why God lets these experiences come. What

108

such troubles will mean will be determined by our attitude, by the way in which we receive and handle them.

Do you think of yourself as a child of God and that you are never alone? The fact is that if a person lives his life alone, and his only confidence is in himself, when trouble befalls that person is disconsolate. He begins to have the feeling that he is being punished, and he is inclined to be resentful about it. He will have a feeling of self-pity in the matter. Everything that happens to him seems to be wrong. He will have the feeling that God is just not fair and he is being crushed under the heavy burden of carrying the whole load.

But when a person thinks of himself as a child of God, and if he lives in the Lord in faith, he will know that God is watching over him. If something happens to him that is not pleasant he will understand this to be permitted by God as a form of chastening. The difference between chastening and punishing is profound. Chastening is done to bring out something good, and the believer can be confident that if he suffers he shall also reign with Him. What, then, is the danger that believers face when they have trouble? That is what this book deals with at this point. The danger is that when believers encounter trouble they are prone to mistake it for punishment. This would be the natural man's view — the unbeliever's view. It should have no place in the mind of a believer.

Someone might at this point ask: "Didn't it hurt?" Yes, it hurt. "Were you not in trouble?" Yes, in a certain sense. Shall we say such troubles came to you from God? Yes, as with all things they came from God. But right here the question is: Did they come as punishment from God or as chastening from God? Someone might say: "I don't see how you can expect good from suffering. If I am having real suffering there seems to be little evidence that God is taking care of me." That would be the way a person would talk if when he was hurt by his dentist he threatened never to return. Would that be wise? Of course the dentist may hurt the tooth; he may even cause it to ache more for the moment, but we trust that what he does will give eventual relief from pain.

As we think about this problem spiritually, consider that when the Heavenly Father looks down upon His children and sees them enmeshed in this world on all sides, He can see how easily they could become attached to this world. Human beings could become so attached to this world they would never want to leave it. They could be more interested in the help of men than in the help of God, more concerned with the goodwill of man than with the blessings of God. In this situation the Heavenly Father moves to help His children; in a sense He wants to wean them from this world. God does this by letting them suffer here. When chastening comes it causes believers to take another view of this world in which they are having so much sorrow. When chastening, sorrow and tribulation come, we can be sure they come for a good purpose.

> If ye endure chastening, God dealeth with you as with sons; for what son is he whom the father chasteneth not? (Heb. 12:7).

If the believer feels he is being subjected to certain suffering he could look to God, wondering what God wants to do with him. He need have no question in his mind that God is doing this, and if we appreciate our earthly parents when they discipline us, how much more shall he appreciate the Holy Spirit of God.

> Furthermore we have had fathers of our flesh which corrected us, and we gave them reverence: shall we not much rather be in subjection unto the Father of spirits, and live? For they verily for a few days chastened us after their own pleasure; but he for our profit, that we might be partakers of his holiness (Heb. 12:9-10).

Our parents disciplined us because they wanted to help us; they had our welfare at heart. How much more would God be concerned for the welfare of His own. God does everything for their benefit, that they might be partakers of His holiness.

> Now no chastening for the present seemeth to be joyous, but grievous: nevertheless afterward it yieldeth the peaceable fruit of righteousness unto them which are exercised thereby (Heb. 12:11).

Some people are exercised by their suffering — others are not. Some people stiffen up, and will not yield to God. Some resent the suffering and these resist God, while others accept the suffering as from God. These believers look up into the face of God and wonder what God has in mind, but they trust God in any case. It is true: "No chastening for the present seemeth joyous." Of course, suffering will hurt; it will cause pain and sorrow. Nevertheless, afterwards it "yieldeth the peaceable fruit of righteousness unto them which are exercised thereby," (if it really made a difference to you).

Always remember, with reference to chastening, that the Father wants to free His children from this world in order that they can turn to Him and receive His blessing.

Chapter 37

THE FUNCTION OF GRACE

Do you know what it means to receive the grace of God?

> Wherefore we receiving a kingdom which cannot be moved, let us have grace, whereby we may serve God acceptably with reverence and godly fear: for our God is a consuming fire (Heb. 12:28-29).

What does it mean about believers having the grace of God? This can be clearly seen in the admonition given by the writer.

> Wherefore lift up the hands which hang down, and the feeble knees; and make straight paths for your feet, lest that which is lame be turned out of the way; but let it rather be healed (Heb. 12:12-13).

A person can get tired so that his natural strength will give away. He no longer will feel disposed to do the will of God. "Lift up the hands which hang down"; the grace of God gives him the strength to do this. The grace of God is God's enablement that will give the believer the strength to lift up the hands in prayer, even beyond his natural strength, and when he no longer would have courage to do this. In other words, God will give each believer the inward capacity to serve Him. "And make straight paths for your feet, lest that which is lame be turned out of the way; but let it rather be healed." The believer should set a good example. He should not deviate, should not wander aimlessly. He should be straightforward with those who are not as strong as he is. In this Scripture we see how man's weakness and God's grace are to be seen together. The believer may in his human nature have the disposition to be worn out and frightened at his prospects, but by the grace of God he can make straight paths for his feet. The believer is led to walk in the open and plain daylight, "lest that which is lame be turned out of the way." The believer should think of the weak ones who are following him, that they might be healed.

> Follow peace with all men, and holiness, without which no man
> shall see the Lord (Heb. 12:14).

Following peace with all men will mean that in any situation the believer
will be given the grace to say nothing or to give a soft answer which turns
away wrath. He will be given grace in his heart to seek peace so that when
he has contention of any sort he is enabled to follow peace with all men.
The believer will make it his ambition to know peace and holiness,
without which no man shall see the Lord. He is to seek as far as possible to
live without contention and strife and he is to be entirely given over to
Christ. "Looking diligently lest any man fail of the grace of God" (Heb.
12:15). It is the grace of God that will enable him to seek peace with all
men and to seek holiness. The believer receives grace from Christ, which
will be strength from Him to do His will. The believer should look
diligently lest he fail of the grace of God.

The writer sets forth his meaning even more plainly:

> Looking diligently lest any man fail of the grace of God; lest any
> root of bitterness springing up trouble you, and thereby many be
> defiled; lest there be any fornicator, or profane person, as Esau, who
> for one morsel of meat sold his birthright (Heb. 12:15-16).

Esau was a person who did not practice self-denial. He ruined himself
personally because of this failure to do God's will. If he had had the grace
of God in his heart he could have denied himself and sought the blessing
which comes only from God, but he was not able to do that. He had not
personally yielded himself to God; so he was in this respect not depending
upon God.

Hebrews 12:18-24 may seem obscure in meaning, but the message
seems plain: "Get serious." Everything in relation to God is extremely
serious. A careful reading of those verses will convey the thought that the
believer in Christ is not coming to Mount Sinai, (as Israel did in the days
of Moses), with its lightning and thunder and in threat of danger, but he is
coming to the city of the living God, the heavenly Jerusalem.

> To the general assembly and church of the firstborn, which are
> written in heaven, and to God the Judge of all, and to the spirits of
> just men made perfect, (a description of all those in heaven); and to
> Jesus the mediator of the new covenant, and to the blood of sprin-
> kling, that speaketh better things than that of Abel. (Heb. 12:23-24).

This is the final contrast of the two covenants.

The believer puts his trust in the living Lord Jesus Christ, raised from
the dead and seated in heavenly places with Almighty God. As the

believer thinks these things over he is to commit himself to Christ with full confidence that God will keep him when he trust in Him.

> See that ye refuse not him that speaketh. For if they escaped not who refused him that spake on earth, much more shall not we escape, if we turn away from him that speaketh from heaven (Heb. 12:25).

The believer is to be very careful — he must not turn away from the message. The writer speaks of how eternal is this God who speaks from heaven. For one thing, He speaks in the Bible. He speaks through the Lord Jesus Christ in both His earthly and heavenly careers. And He speaks by the Holy Spirit. Believers have inner guidance that leads them toward God. God also speaks in circumstances and in providence as things happen. The call is to believers to put their trust in the Lord Jesus Christ; they are to be careful not to refuse Him that speaketh because this could be dangerous.

> Wherefore we receiving a kingdom which cannot be moved, let us have grace, whereby we may serve God acceptably with reverence and godly fear: for our God is a consuming fire (Heb. 12:28-29).

Believers need the grace of God in their hearts and they need to understand what Christ will do. Believers need to understand what the Lord has planned. When they have believed and put their faith in Him, they need to look to God that they might serve Him acceptably, because this is part of the whole plan. When believers yield themselves to the Lord Jesus Christ, He will work out His will in them by guiding them so that they can serve Him acceptably by faith. Without faith it is impossible to please Him. The faith the believer needs, the inner disposition to please God, is the result of the grace of God in his heart which God gives to him.

Chapter 38

THE LIFE OF FAITH

Do you think there would be anything wrong in following the faith of other believers?

> Whose faith follow, considering the end of their conversation. Jesus Christ the same yesterday, and today, and for ever (Heb. 13:7-8).

We have been studying this epistle to the Hebrews in order to learn as well as we can what it has to tell us about the salvation which is in Jesus Christ. We have learned that God has provided blessing for believers in Jesus Christ, and the greatest blessing possible is that which comes when a person believes in Him. Much of this is a matter of the mind — of understanding the gospel. In a very real sense the gospel does not become operative until the person acts upon it. The sinner should try to understand as well as he can, and the understanding must then be put into performance. So there is always a practical purpose in the study of the gospel. All deliberations and all reflections lead into clearer understanding, a better idea of what the believer can and should do in Christ Jesus.

The gospel moves within an orbit that embraces both earth and heaven. The fact is that God is up there and the sinner is down here, and there is a connection between the two. The first revelation that comes to the soul is that of the law of God — what God requires. The believer learns that God is holy, just and good. As the believer comes to know the nature of God, the Creator of all things, he learns something about the nature of creation. In creation it is also true there is integrity, honesty, straightforwardness and reliability. All of this is revealed in the law of Moses, commonly called the Ten Commandments. When anyone studies the Ten Commandments he can see in them plainly what God requires of man.

God being what He is, what does that mean to man? To know this, one should read the Ten Commandments. In the Old Testament the grace of God is to be seen in the tabernacle. When a man broke one of the

114

commandments, that which he must do for penitence was set forth in the ritual of the tabernacle. This is the first revelation. It is referred to in this epistle as "the first covenant." This could also be called "the old covenant." It is the truth that is revealed through Moses. The book of Hebrews especially emphasizes the further, deeper, and more significant revelation of the gospel as seen in Christ Jesus, who obeyed the law and made it possible for believers to join Him in their faith in the life He now lives since the resurrection. Believers can join the Lord Jesus Christ as He is today. This is revealed in the gospel, which is the truth as it is in Christ Jesus.

This living in Christ, having fellowship with Him, is possible only when a believer responds to God in faith. God reveals the promises and tells what He will do. The believer responds to Him and God will make His promise real and actual in that life. The believer needs help in order to believe. He may hear what is to be done, but how can he believe it? For that he needs the grace of God. He needs help to walk in faith in Christ Jesus. He may see how the Lord Jesus Christ walks and he may see how He denies Himself. The believer may see how He walks through Gethsemane going to Calvary in order to do the will of God. How will it be possible for the believer to decide within himself that he wants to go that way? This happens by the grace of God that He will give to anyone if he is willing. This is what makes it possible for a sinner to believe in Christ, to obey Him, and to really yield himself to follow Him.

Hebrews 13:1-8 shows how faith enables a believer to walk in the ways of the Lord. In order for brotherly love to continue day in and day out the believer needs the grace of God, because in brotherly love it will be in the heart of the believer to be concerned about the other man, not himself. That is not natural; it is spiritual. It is God who enables the believer to do that, because that is in the nature of God.

> Be not forgetful to entertain strangers: for thereby some have entertained angels unawares (Heb. 13:2).

Here is guidance in the direction of hospitality. When a person entertains strangers, what does that mean? It means he opens his heart, his home, his purse, his thoughts and his fellowship to welcome people he has not known. Such strangers are not part of his personal program, but he will entertain them. He will be kind and gracious to them. How can he do this? When the believer has the grace of God in his heart he will remember the strangers are God's people, and since they are God's people, they have a claim upon him. The writer says that some have entertained angels unawares. This reminds us how Abraham and Sarah prepared a meal for strangers who came to them. Those strangers turned out to be angels from

God. This is a challenge for all believers to remember they never know whom they are dealing with. The believer should not be isolated within his own circle of friends, but he should be openhearted toward all people. Some to whom he opens his heart may turn out to be those who will bring him blessing from God.

> Remember them that are in bonds, as bound with them; and them which suffer adversity, as being yourselves also in the body (Heb. 13:3).

The believer should have sympathy toward people who are in trouble. Those in bonds are those who are in jail. The believer should think of them as if he were bound with them. The believer should think of those who "suffer adversity," those who are having trouble, and should remember trouble could happen to him.

> Marriage is honorable in all, and the bed undefiled: but whoremongers and adulterers God will judge (Heb. 13:4).

This is a very personal word; it emphasizes that God requires integrity in personal relations. Carelessness and looseness in personal affairs are unacceptable to God.

> Let your conversation be without covetousness; and be content with such things as ye have: for he hath said, I will never leave thee, nor forsake thee (Heb. 13:5).

The believer should not always be trying to get something for himself. He can have contentment, a wonderful blessing, by the grace of God; he will understand that God will take care of him.

> So that we may boldly say, The Lord is my helper, and I will not fear what man shall do unto me (Heb. 13:6).

It is possible to have real confidence in God.

> Remember them which have the rule over you, who have spoken unto you the word of God: whose faith follow, considering the end of their conversation (Heb. 13:7).

The believer should show honor to those who teach the gospel and who preach the gospel, and should have respect for those who have gone before in the faith of the Lord Jesus Christ. He should follow them, remembering all things that are done in the name of the Lord Jesus Christ. This kind of living is possible when you have the grace of God in your heart.

Chapter 39

WALKING WITH CHRIST
AROUSES HOSTILE OPPOSITION

If a man were to accept Christ and begin to live in the will of God, do you think he would win approval from other people?

Jesus Christ is the very heart of the gospel. All the promises of God center in Him. In these studies attention has been focused constantly upon Jesus Christ. From the very first chapter of this epistle the writer has continually brought his readers face to face with the things of the Lord Jesus Christ and has shown that in Him is the highest possible blessing a believer can have from God. In the last chapter the emphasis was upon action that is required of us. Sometimes it seems that insofar as spiritual experience is concerned a believer should get his ideas straightened out, get the right doctrine in his mind, and be sure he thinks and says the right things. Then he should go out and do and act as he sees fit, doing the best he can. There always seems to be a big gap between what the person believes and what he does. It is not intended to be that way.

Believers are to understand what God has offered to them in Christ Jesus. Through their understanding they come to know what God intends they should believe in Christ. Believing in Christ will cause certain results to follow in their daily lives so that in their actions which follow they will be doing and acting in accord with what they believe about the Lord Jesus Christ. All that believers seek they are to find in Him. All that they will depend upon, they will find in Christ Jesus. All that believers have is in the living Lord Jesus Christ.

"Be not carried about with divers and strange doctrines" (Heb. 13:9). This is a way of saying "avoid unusual, strange ideas." Every now and then there are sincere, earnest believers who are truly desirous of pleasing the Lord. They may have taken a public stand for Christ and may have openly witnessed and testified that they belong to Him, but who then seem to develop strange ideas and odd notions. Perhaps they think that being a believer is in itself so peculiar that anything really strange can be characteristic of Christianity. But the truth is not quite like that. It is true that being a believer is remarkable. It is also true that living the spiritual life is extraordinary, but it is not strange and peculiar after all.

> For it is a good thing that the heart be established with grace; not with meats, which have not profited them that have been occupied therein (Heb. 13:9).

Believers should be strengthened by the grace of God, not by any particular thing they think or do. Some people develop strange procedures when they become believers. There are things they will do and things they will not do. Because they are believers they emphasize that this personal habit is right and that personal habit is wrong. Believers who do that are referred to in this passage as those who are involved with "meats."

Being occupied with "meat" is being occupied with what a believer should eat and what he should not eat, where he should go and where he should not go, what he should do and should not do. This line of emphasis is not truly profitable. The believer should be established with grace in his heart from the Lord; then he will have daily strength from Christ to obey Him at all times — doing what he has to do in the name of the Lord Jesus Christ. This is far more important than having a set of rules.

> We have an altar, whereof they have no right to eat which serve the tabernacle. For the bodies of those beasts, whose blood is brought into the sanctuary by the high priest for sin, are burned without the camp. Wherefore Jesus also, that he might sanctify the people with his own blood, suffered without the gate (Heb. 13:10-12).

These verses indicate something which in our time believers usually do not know about. This passage refers to matters you and I would not learn about in our culture. To understand this it is necessary to know the history of the Old Testament. In the Old Testament, in the days of the Levites and in the days of the tabernacle, it was the custom that when the priest brought in a sin offering and the blood was shed, the animal was burned outside the camp, away from where the people were. Actually, in our time we would say out on the dump heap. This writer is saying here that is where believers belong. That is where Jesus of Nazareth died. He suffered for sinners "outside the gate." He was repudiated, treated like refuse. He was put to death on Calvary's cross, set upon the hill called Golgotha. That was the city's dump heap. Here the writer is saying that since Jesus of Nazareth experienced this rejection and was put away from everybody else to be repudiated and rejected, believers should willingly join Him there.

Let us go forth therefore unto him without the camp, bearing his reproach. For here have we no continuing city, but we seek one to come (Heb. 13:13-14).

The believer is to go forth without human approval, sharing the rejection that came to Jesus of Nazareth. Here is something that is true, but not easy to bear. When a believer puts his trust in the Lord Jesus Christ he finds in a rather strange way that people will give him the short end of the stick, so to speak. The public will repudiate him. It is hard to understand why others should be so hostile toward anyone who is seeking to do the will of God, but as surely as a believer puts his trust in Christ Jesus he can expect to be accorded this treatment. The writer here is saying in spite of such prospect, do it — let the believer go forth unto Him outside the camp, away from human approval, bearing His reproach.

In this world the believer will not have the fullness of blessing. He seeks blessing in the future, so he follows Him into disrepute. Human beings have made one simple issue out of the whole matter that involves the gospel: Either a man will serve the things which please self, or he shall walk with the Lord Jesus Christ. No man is going to do both. He will either do what pleases self or he will do what pleases Christ. Most people do what pleases themselves. As is often said concerning an attitude like this: "me, my wife, my son, John, and his wife; us four, no more." That is usually the way it is with the natural person.

Those who follow after Christ seek His will and His approval. Most people who are selfish are actually hostile to those who follow Christ. That is the way Ishmael was with Isaac, and that is the way Cain was with Abel when he killed him. Those who are after the flesh will persecute those who are after the Spirit.

Chapter 40

THE RESURRECTION OF CHRIST JESUS
PROMISES BLESSING TO THE BELIEVER

Have you any idea what a believer should be thinking about all the time?

By him therefore let us offer the sacrifice of praise to God continually, that is, the fruit of our lips giving thanks to his name (Heb. 13:15).

The epistle to the Hebrews has been discussing the various matters involved in receiving the fullness of blessing which is in Christ Jesus. This epistle started out to lead the reader to understand that there is more blessing available in Christ Jesus than there is in trying to keep the rules and regulations as to what is right and wrong. Far beyond knowing what to do, is the matter of knowing Christ who will help the believer to do as he should. In this last study, in the final verses of chapter 13, one theme was prominent: Praise belongs to God.

Enter into his gates with thanksgiving, and into his courts with praise: be thankful unto him, and bless his name (Ps. 100:4).

The writer urges that one worthy of personal relationship with God, and the experience of the grace of God, is one who thanks Him and praises Him. God is blessing His people always. God has provided in Christ Jesus not only for times of emergency and not only for times of special need, but for all times. So believers should praise Him always. There will be times when the believer feels fortunate and everything is going fine — at which time praise is easy — but there will also be times when he is not fortunate, when he suffers. There will be times when the believer has distress, such as when the believer is associated with Christ and is repudiated by others. When the believer wants to be well pleasing in the sight of God he is not appreciated by other men. At such times he is actually criticized and others will take advantage of him. He may be left alone many times. In all of this, according to this Scripture, the believer is encouraged to praise God for His goodness and mercy.

These studies in Hebrews will enable the reader to understand how the blessing of God is received. Here can be learned the wonderful truth that all that is necessary for blessing from God has been provided in Christ Jesus. He makes it available. Believers receive it from Him by faith. Believers trust in Him and Christ works in them that which is well pleasing in His sight. This epistle helps the believer to understand that he no longer needs to strive in his own efforts, or to struggle as if he were going to try to accomplish things, but he only needs to yield to Christ and He will work these things out for him.

In this last portion of the book different points are set forth which should be kept in mind as to how the believer can trust Him. Here are stated some of the things a believer should do as he lives in the Lord Jesus Christ, strengthened by the grace of God; i.e. "by Him" (because of Christ Jesus in him, he will find inwardly that he will be moved to praise and thank God). Sometimes the believer can see, but when he cannot see, he can trust and he can always know that God is good, and he can praise Him for the things He has done.

> But to do good and to communicate forget not: for with such sacrifices God is well pleased (Heb. 13:16).

In addition to thanking and praising God, the believer should do good. He should help the poor, obey those in authority and respect God. He should make it a point to worship God in public. He should give of his means and his time. Instead of just bringing sacrifices to the Lord, he should take them to other people. This pleases Almighty God.

> Obey them that have the rule over you, and submit yourselves: for they watch for your souls, as they that must give account, that they may do it with joy, and not with grief: for that is unprofitable for you (Heb. 13:17).

Here is a word with reference to the believer's fellowship among other believers in the congregation. There are some people who have certain responsibilities. The believer should help them. He should be easy to lead, and ready to submit himself. He should make it easy for those who have the responsibility to lead him. This will be agreeable to God. That is what the Lord Jesus Christ would have done.

> Pray for us: for we trust we have a good conscience, in all things willing to live honestly (Heb. 13:18).

He should pray for other believers, and pray for leaders. He should pray for teachers and for preachers.

> But I beseech you the rather to do this, that I may be restored to you the sooner (Heb. 13:19).

The believer should so pray for the servants of the Lord for a practical reason, not only because it is good but because he himself can receive benefits from it. Thus even today believers should pray for leaders and pastors not only because that is good for the gospel, but also because there will be a blessing upon them. God will not forget that they have been faithful in prayer.

> Now the God of peace, that brought again from the dead our Lord Jesus, that great shepherd of the sheep, through the blood of the everlasting covenant, make you perfect in every good work to do his will, working in you that which is well-pleasing in his sight, through Jesus Christ; to whom be glory for ever and ever. Amen (Heb. 13:20-21).

There is something in the resurrection of the Lord Jesus Christ that opens the way for a believer to be blessed; he can be strengthened because, as the Lord Jesus Christ was raised from the dead, so God will raise him from the dead and make him perfect. God will make him complete, mature. When a believer wonders what is well-pleasing in His sight, he can remember how Almighty God looked down upon the Lord Jesus Christ when He came into this world and said: "This is my beloved Son, in whom I am well pleased."

While the Lord Jesus Christ was here He said: "I do nothing of myself. I do all things to please my Father." That was well pleasing in the sight of the Lord. Again Jesus of Nazareth would say: "Not my will, but thine be done." So the prayer in this benediction is that God make the believer mature, and develop and strengthen him, and make him full grown in every good work to do His will, working in the believer that which is well pleasing in God's sight through Jesus Christ.

The believer needs to remember that is the whole secret of the Christian gospel. He is not working for the Lord. The Lord is working in him, producing in him that which is pleasing in His sight. The closing verses are the usual ending of a simple letter.

I trust that in the study of this book the student has been led more and more to see how everything depends upon the living Lord and Savior, Jesus Christ.